THE BEECHWOOD BOOKS

Edited by

SAMUEL J. LOOKER

CRICKET

Cricket Anthology

Compiled by Samuel J. Looker

SPELLMOUNT LTD.
TUNBRIDGE WELLS, KENT

In the Spellmount Cricket series:
The Test Match Career of Geoffrey Boycott
by C. D. Clark
The Test Match Career of Sir Jack Hobbs by Clive Porter
The Test Match Career of Colin Cowdrey
by Derek Barnard

First published in the UK in 1925 by
Simpkin Marshall, Beechwood Books

Re-printed in the UK in 1988 by
SPELLMOUNT LTD
12 Dene Way, Speldhurst
Tunbridge Wells, Kent TN3 0NX
ISBN 0-946771-52-9
© Spellmount Ltd 1988

British Library Cataloguing in Publication Data
    Cricket anthology
    1. Cricket
    I. Looker, Samuel J. (Samuel Joseph)
    796.35'8
    ISBN 0-946771-52-9

Printed in Great Britain by
Ipswich Book Company Ltd, Ipswich

For

CAROLINE

Who Plays the Game

SONG

WHAT Englishman can dare
Any pastime to compare
With the great and grand old manly game we love ?
What sight so sweet to view
As a wicket hard and true,
And the fieldsmen kept for ever on the move ?

Chorus :

Run, run, run, the ball's a-rolling,
Scarcely to the boundary she'll go ;
And the throwing's getting wild, and the wicket-
keeper's riled,
So we'll try and steal another for the throw.

HORACE G. HUTCHINSON.

FOREWORD

THE Beechwood Books, of which this is the fourth to be issued, are designed to provide lovers of Sporting Literature with a series of little volumes which give a selection from the best books on sport past and present. It has been sought in their compilation, not so much to capture the ephemeral, the fugitive description or incident, as by quoting those extracts which give an authentic and lasting impression of the thing seen and felt to convey the true atmosphere of the game.

The infinite variety of sporting literature offers ample scope to the editor. But the task is not easy. Seldom are books found so ephemeral in content as the average study or novel on sport is apt to prove. Possibly this is not so true of Cricket as of other pastimes, for English literature abounds with vivid and picturesque descriptions of Cricket the King. Of late years a number of excellent Cricket novels have been published, while the cricket verses of Norman Gale and E. B. V. Christian have been deservedly popular.

Cricket during several centuries has passed through many phases. It is difficult to fix with any certainty the date of the first authentic mention of the game in English literature.

One or two scattered references to Cricket may

ix

be found in old records of Elizabeth's time, but these are probably references to a form of stool-ball rather than any variety of the modern game of Cricket. One may agree with Andrew Lang in his informative sketch of the History of Cricket [1] where he ventures the opinion

" Both stool-ball and cat-and-dog have closer affinities with cricket than club-ball, as represented in Strutt's authorities. Perhaps we may say that wherever stool-ball was played, or cat-and-dog, there cricket was potentially present."

In the seventeenth century Cricket was merely a boy's game.

At the beginning of the eighteenth it had achieved a certain dignity and the honour of mention by Mr. Pope. By the end of that century it had its own Laureate and famous players were beginning to be talked about. Even by 1750 heavy bets on the game were the rule and scores were recorded. The Hambledon Club was the rallying point of this old-time vigorous cricket. The giants of this famous club are they not chronicled for all time in the picturesque prose of old John Nyren ? Some striking passages from this writer are quoted in the text. His book possesses perennial charm for lovers of the game.

Underhand bowling was the rule until the early years of the nineteenth century. Then one or two pioneers began to bowl roundhand. The innovation led to a tremendous controversy, echoes of which may be found in the writings of Nyren and Pycroft. The advocates of roundhand bowling ultimately won the day, and about the year 1845 it became a recognized institution.

[1] *Cricket* (The Badminton Library).

The founding of the M.C.C. and its early history are referred to in the body of this book, there is no need therefore to deal with the matter in this place. One may regret in passing, however, as all cricket historians must do, the great fire at Lords' Cricket Ground, which destroyed so many early and irreplaceable records of the game.

As we read in Nyren or Pycroft or rejoice at Felix on the Bat, shades of the giants of the past, and grand echoes of old-time battles are conjured up in memory. And perhaps from thus reading we are led to think of those classic fights of our own time that deserve the pen of a Hazlitt to do them justice ? Yet at long last we may derive consolation from the fact that even as one writes there are giants on the earth making Cricket history.

Much could be said of the charm of the surroundings in which Cricket is played, especially in the country on the village green. The quiet idyllic summer afternoon, the green turf fringed with trees, the ring of earnest onlookers, all combine to furnish a setting of rare beauty and enduring charm,

> O Memory ! shield me from the World's poor strife,
> And give those scenes thine everlasting life !

The tragedy and comedy of village Cricket ! It has been well said that in its best moments there is lyric poetry. Even if one knew nothing of the players one could learn something of them by watching them play.

The literature of Cricket seems to appeal to the moralist. I love the patient kindliness of Charles Cowden Clarke, in his Introduction to *The Young*

Cricketer's Tutor, by John Nyren, published in 1833, his theme is manliness :

Of all the English athletic games, none, perhaps, present so fine a scope for bringing into full and constant play the qualities both of the mind and body as that of Cricket. A man who is essentially stupid will not make a fine cricketer ; neither will he who is not essentially active. He must be active in all his faculties—he must be active in mind to prepare for every advantage, and active in eye and limb, to avail himself of those advantages. He must be cool-tempered, and, in the best sense of the term, Manly ; for he must be able to endure fatigue, and to make light of pain ; since, like all athletic sports, Cricket is not unattended with danger, resulting from inattention or inexperience ; the accidents most commonly attendant upon the players at Cricket arising from unwatchfulness, or slowness of eye.

A short-sighted person is as unfit to become a cricketer, as one deaf would be to discriminate the most delicate graduations and varieties in tones ; added to which, he must be in constant jeopardy of serious injury.

Painstaking prose, yet pleasing enough in its way.

Effective, too, is the quaint moralizing of James Pycroft, one of the classic writers on Cricket,[1] who in the following passages writes with much point on the spirit of the game :

There is something highly intellectual in our noble and national pastime. But the cricketer must possess certain qualifications, not only physical and intellectual, but moral qualifications also ; for of what avail is the mind to design and the hand to execute, if a sulky temper paralyses his exertions and throws a damp upon the field ; or if impatience dethrones judgment, and the man hits across at good balls, because loose balls are long in coming ; or, again, if a contentious and imperious disposition leaves the cricketer all " alone in his glory," voted the pest of every eleven.

The pest of the cricket-field is the man who bores you about his average—his wickets—his catches, and looks blue even at the success of his own party. Give me the man who forgets himself in the game, and, missing a ball, does not stop to excul-

---

[1] J. Pycroft, *The Cricket Field* [1851].

pate himself by dumb show, but rattles away after it—who does not blame his partner when he is run out.

If such a man makes a score, players remark on all sides, "Our friend deserves luck for his good humour and true spirit of the game."

Add to all this, perseverance and self-denial, and a soul above vainglory and the applause of the vulgar.

Conceit in a cricketer, as in other things, is a bar to all improvement—the vain player is always thinking of the lookers-on instead of the game, and generally is condemned to live on the reputation of one shying leg-hit, or some twenty runs off three or four overs (his merriest life is a short one) for half a season.

In one word, there is no game in which amiability and an unruffled temper is so essential to success, or in which virtue is rewarded half as much as in the game of Cricket.

I love also the description of a village cricket match by Miss Mitford, in *Our Village*, equally with the essay by Leigh Hunt in *The Seer, or, Commonplaces Refreshed*,[1] where he writes :—

It would be a pretty world, if we all had something to do, just to make leisure the pleasanter, and green merry England were sprinkled all over "of afternoons" with gallant fellows in white sleeves, who threshed the earth and air of their cricket-grounds into a crop of health and spirits ; after which they should read, laugh, love, and be honourable and happy beings, bringing God's work to its perfection, and suiting the divine creation they live in. . . . Nature is stirring and so is the cricketer. Nature, in a hundred thousand parts to a fraction, is made up of air, and fields, and country, and out-of-doors, and a strong teeming earth, and a good-natured sky ; and so is the strong heart of the cricketer.[2]

There is some admirable cricket lore in *Uncle John* by G. J. Whyte-Melville, which I discovered too late to include in the body of this book. I should have liked also to have quoted the cricket verses by Francis

---

[1] *The Seer, on Cricket and Exercise in General.* By Leigh Hunt.

[2] Possibly cricket was invented by a thoughtful Providence to minister to the happiness of Harold Skimpole.

Thompson which come so strangely from that erratic and unathletic genius.

Among present-day writers none are more effective on the subject of Cricket than Sir James Barrie. In a speech made at Dundee on May 5th, 1922, Sir James told several amusing stories about his own early cricketing days. He said he once set out with a team of well-known people to whom he had to teach the game while they were in the train. One man who kept saying, " Intellect succeeds in the end," was caught first ball by the local curate, while a scholastic member of his team said to him : " Should I strike the ball, to however small an extent, I shall run with considerable velocity."

One hears a good deal nowadays about women and sport, and fair cricketers are much to the front, yet this is no new thing after all. The *Sporting Magazine,* under date December 22nd, 1792, reports the following :

A very curious match of cricket was played by eleven girls of Rotherby, Leicestershire, against an equal number of Hoby, on Thursday, on their feast-week. The inhabitants of all the villages adjacent were eager spectators of this novel and interesting contest ; when, after a display of astonishing feats of skill and activity, the palm of victory was obtained by the fair maidens of Rotherby. There are about ten houses in Rotherby, and near sixty in Hoby ; so great a disproportion affords matter of exultation to the honest rustics of the first mentioned village. The bowlers of the conquering party were immediately placed in a sort of triumphal car, preceded by music and flying streamers, and thus conducted home by the youths of Rotherby, amidst the acclamations of a numerous group of pleased spectators.

So one might continue to browse amid the old-time literature of Cricket striving to rescue from

Time," the ever swift," something of past joys and battles long ago ; for is it not possible to find in such recreation rest and refreshment in our own feverish and conceited age.

As to present day writers on Cricket, most of them figure in the text of this anthology. But reasons of copyright and so forth prevent one or two from being so represented. Among such, high rank must be accorded to Neville Cardus, whose *A Cricketer's Book* seems to me one of the best books ever written on the game.

Some excellent Cricket novels have been written by novelists of to-day. Extracts from several of these appear in the text, but I recall among others *The Cricket Match* by Hugh de Selincourt, *Psmith* by P. G. Wodehouse, and stories by Desmond Coke, which are equally fine and worthy of mention.

The late E. W. Hornung, the creator of Raffles, was an enthusiastic cricketer and wrote on his favourite game with much charm and humour.

In that fine Gothic romance *Desolate Splendour*, by Michael Sadleir, is a description of an Oxford and Cambridge match which is worthy of Trollope, although among all his admirable sporting scenes I am not aware that Anthony ever actually described a match.

Football enthralls its millions, and tennis its thousands, but Cricket remains the real King of Games, with its specially English appeal and standard of honour. Neither football with its occasional rowdyism and vulgarity, nor tennis, with its irritatingly-frequent stupid hero worship of flannelled fools and agile legs, and the ubiquitous and trivial photograph, may compete with it on equal terms.

The love of Cricket is an integral part of the English spirit. It is part of that unique and compelling force of character and achievement which has made our island race the pioneers of discovery in strange lands and the founders of empire beyond the sea. While this love of manly pastime endures we need not fear for the future. On the playing fields of England the youth of England learn endurance and courage, and how to play the game in every sense of the word. In Cricket personal emulation plays a part it is true, but more than individual self-seeking is the spirit of playing for the side. It has been well said that without fine bowling, fine batting is impossible, in the same way Cricket encourages a true sporting spirit among its players, and has been in the past and is now less open to the abuses which creep into other sports.

Little remains to be said. It has been the Editor's pleasant task to linger for awhile amid the shades of the past, to glean ears of corn in old fields. The game has seen many changes, has experienced many ups and downs, but there is no reason to doubt that it is as firmly established to-day in the affections of its votaries as at any time in its long and glorious history.

SAMUEL J. LOOKER.

SOUTH GREEN, BILLERICAY.
August 10th, 1924.

CONTENTS

PAGE

Contents

CRICKET IN THE PAST

Contents

Contents   xxiii

Contents XXV

Contents xxvii

ACKNOWLEDGMENTS

THE Editor desires to thank the following Authors and Publishers for their courtesy in granting permission to quote various copyright extracts :

This book was prepared slightly over four years ago, but circumstances have prevented its publication until now. A word of apology for the long delay in publication is therefore due.

Mr. Norman Gale, Mr. P. F. Warner, Mr. E. B. V. Christian [*At the Sign of the Wicket*].

Mr. H. A. Vachell [*The Hill*] and Mr. John Murray.

Mr. W. M. Meredith [for an extract from *Evan Harrington* by George Meredith] and Constable & Co.

Mr. G. F. Wilson [*Cricket Poems*].

Mr. J. C. Snaith [*Willow the King*] and Messrs. Ward, Lock & Co.

Mr. E. Phillips Oppenheim [*The Missioner*], Messrs. Methuen, Grant Richards and Longmans Green & Co., and William Blackwood & Sons.

CRICKET

HAMBLEDON MEN

Broad Halfpenny ∽ ∽ ∽ ∽

THERE was high feasting held on Broad Halfpenny
during the solemnity of one of our grand matches.
Oh! it was a heart-stirring sight to witness the
multitude forming a complete and dense circle
round that noble green. Half the county would
be present, and all their hearts with us—Little
Hambledon, pitted against All England was a proud
thought for the Hampshire men. Defeat was
glory in such a struggle—victory, indeed, made us
only 'a little lower than angels.' How those fine
brawn-faced fellows of farmers would drink to our
success! And then, what stuff they had to drink!
Punch—not your new Ponche à la Romaine, or
Ponche à la Groseille, or your modern cat-lap milk-
punch—punch be-devilled; but good, unsophisti-
cated, John Bull stuff—stark!—that would stand
on end—punch that would make a cat speak!
Sixpence a bottle!

The ale too!—not the modern horror under that
name, that drives as many men melancholy-mad
as the hypocrites do—not the beastliness of these
days, that will make a fellow's inside like a shaking

bog, and as rotten ; but barley-corn, such as would put the souls of three butchers into one weaver. Ale that would flare like turpentine—genuine Boniface !—This immortal viand (for it was more than liquor) was vended at twopence per pint. The immeasurable villainy of our vintners would, with their march of intellect (if ever they could get such a brewing), drive a pint of it out into a gallon. Then the quantity the fellows would eat ! Two or three of them would strike dismay into a round of beef. They could no more have pecked in that style than they could have flown, had the infernal black stream (that type of Acheron !) which soddens the carcass of a Londoner, been the fertilizer of their clay. There would this company, consisting most likely of some thousands, remain patiently and anxiously watching every turn of fate in the game, as if the event had been the meeting of two armies to decide their liberty. And whenever a Hambledon man made a good hit, worth four or five runs, you would hear the deep mouths of the whole multitude baying away in pure Hampshire —' Go hard !—go hard !—Tich and turn !—tich and turn ! ' To the honour of my countrymen, let me bear testimony upon this occasion also, as I have already done upon others. Although their provinciality in general, and personal partialities individually, were naturally interested in behalf of the Hambledon men, I cannot call to recollection an instance of their wilfully stopping a ball that had been hit out among them by one of our opponents. Like true Englishmen, they would give an enemy fair play. How strongly are all those scenes of fifty years by-gone, painted in my memory !—

and the smell of that ale comes upon me as freshly
as the new May flowers.

JOHN NYREN.

Tom Sueter ⌀ ⌀ ⌀ ⌀ ⌀

. . . THE name and figure of Tom Sueter first
comes across me—a Hambledon man, and of the
club. What a handful of steel-hearted soldiers are
in an important pass, such was Tom in keeping
the wicket. Nothing went by him, and for coolness and nerve in this trying and responsible post,
I never saw his equal. As a proof of his quickness and skill, I have numberless times seen him
stump a man out with Brett's tremendous bowling.
Add to this valuable accomplishment, he was one
of the manliest and most graceful of hitters. Few
would cut a ball harder at the point of the bat,
and he was, moreover, an excellent short runner.
He had an eye like an eagle—rapid and compre-
hensive. He was the first who departed from the
custom of the old players before him, who deemed
it a heresy to leave the crease for the ball ; he
would get in at it, and hit it straight off and straight
on, and, egad ! it went as if it had been fired. As
by the rules of our club, at the trial-matches no
man was allowed to get more than thirty runs, he
generally gained his number earlier than any of
them. I have seldom seen a handsomer man than
Tom Sueter, who measured about five feet ten.
As if, too, Dame Nature wished to show at his
birth a specimen of her prodigality, she gave him
so amiable a disposition that he was the pet of all

the neighbourhood ; so honourable a heart, that his word was never questioned by the gentlemen who associated with him ; and a voice, which for sweetness, power and purity of tone (a tenor), would, with proper cultivation, have made him a handsome fortune.   With what rapture have I hung upon his notes when he has given us a hunting song in the club-room after the day's practice was over !

JOHN NYREN.

George Lear ⌒ ⌒ ⌒ ⌒ ⌒

GEORGE LEAR, of Hambledon, who always answered to the title among us of ' Little George,' was our best long-stop. So firm and steady was he, that I have known him stand through a whole match against Brett's bowling and not lose more than two runs. The ball seemed to go into him, and he was as sure of it as if he had been a sandbank. His activity was so great, and, besides, he had so good a judgment in running to cover the ball, that he would stop many that were hit in the slip, and this, be it remembered, from the swiftest bowling ever known. The portion of ground that man would cover was quite extraordinary. He was a good batsman, and a tolerably sure guard of his wicket ; he averaged from fifteen to twenty runs, but I never remember his having a long innings. What he did not bring to the stock by his bat, however, he amply made up with his perfect fielding. Lear was a short man, of a fair complexion, well-looking, and of a pleasing aspect. He had a sweet counter-tenor voice. Many a treat have I

had in hearing him and Sueter join in a glee at the
' Bat and Ball ' on Broad Halfpenny :

> " I have been there, and still would go ;
> 'Twas like a little heaven below ! "

JOHN NYREN.

Lambert ◇ ◇ ◇ ◇ ◇ ◇

HE was a bowler—right-handed, and he had the
most extraordinary delivery I ever saw. The ball
was delivered quite low, and with a twist ; not like
that of the generality of right-handed bowlers, but
just the reverse way : that is, if bowling to a right-
handed hitter, his ball would twist from the off
stump into the leg. He was the first I remember
who introduced this deceitful and teasing style of
delivering the ball. When All England played the
Hambledon Club, the Little Farmer (Lambert) was
appointed one of our bowlers, and, egad ! this new
trick of his so bothered the Kent and Surrey men,
that they tumbled out one after another, as if they
had been picked off by a rifle corps. For a long
time they could not tell what to make of that
cursed twist of his. This, however, was the only
virtue he possessed as a cricketer. He was no
batter, and had no judgment of the game.

JOHN NYREN.

Richard Nyren ◇ ◇ ◇ ◇

RICHARD NYREN was left-handed. He had a high
delivery, always to the length, and his balls were
provokingly deceitful. He was the chosen general

of all the matches, ordering and directing the whole. In such esteem did the brotherhood hold his experience and judgment, that he was uniformly consulted on all questions of law or precedent, and I never knew an exception to be taken against his opinion, or his decision to be reversed. I never saw a finer specimen of the thorough-bred old English yeoman than Richard Nyren. He was a good face-to-face, unflinching, uncompromising, independent man. He placed a full and just value upon the station he held in society, and he maintained it without insolence or assumption. He could differ with a superior without trenching upon his dignity or losing his own. I have known him maintain an opinion with great firmness against the Duke of Dorset and Sir Horace Mann, and when, in consequence of his being proved to be in the right, the latter has afterwards crossed the ground and shaken him heartily by the hand. Nyren had immense advantage over Brett ; for, independently of his general knowledge of the game, he was practically a better cricketer, being a safe batsman and an excellent hitter. Although a very stout man (standing about five feet nine) he was uncommonly active. He owed all the skill and judgment he possessed to an old uncle, Richard Newland, of Slindon, in Sussex, under whom he was brought up—a man so famous in his time, that when a song was written in honour of the Sussex cricketers, Richard Newland was especially and honourably signalized. No one man ever dared to play him. When Richard Nyren left Hambledon, the club broke up and never resumed from that day. The head and right arm were gone. JOHN NYREN.

David Harris ∽   ∽   ∽   ∽   ∽

IT would be difficult, perhaps impossible, to convey in writing an accurate idea of the grand effect of Harris's bowling ; they only who have played against him can fully appreciate it.   This attitude, when preparing for his run previously to delivering the ball, would have made a beautiful study for the sculptor.   Phidias would certainly have taken him for a model.   First of all, he stood erect like a soldier at drill ; then, with a graceful curve of the arm, he raised the ball to his forehead, and drawing back his right foot, started off with his left.   The calm look and general air of the man were uncommonly striking, and from this series of preparations he never deviated.   I am sure that from this simple account of his manner, all my countrymen who were acquainted with his play will recall him to their minds.   His mode of delivering the ball was very singular.   He would bring it from under the arm by a twist, and nearly as high as his arm-pit, and with this action *push* it, as it were, from him. How it was that the balls acquired the velocity they did by this mode of delivery, I never could comprehend.

When first he joined the Hambledon Club, he was quite a raw countryman at cricket, and had very little to recommend him but his noble delivery. He was also very apt to give tosses.   I have seen old Nyren scratch his head and say : ' Harris would make the best bowler in England if he did not toss.'   By continual practice, however, and following the advice of the old Hambledon players, he became as steady as could be wished, and in

the prime of his playing very rarely indeed gave a
toss, although his balls were pitched the full length.
In bowling, he never stooped in the least in his
delivery, but kept himself upright all the time.
His balls were very little beholden to the ground
when pitched ; it was but a touch and up again,
and woe be to the man who did not get in to
block them, for they had such a peculiar curl
that they would grind his fingers against the
bat; many a time have I seen the blood drawn
in this way from a batter who was not up to
the trick.

Harris's bowling was the finest of all tests for a
batter, and hence the great beauty, as I observed
before, of seeing Beldham in with this man against
him ; for unless a batter were of the very first
class, and accustomed to the first style of stopping,
he could do–little or nothing with Harris. If the
thing had been possible, I should have liked to
have seen such a player as Budd (fine hitter as he
was) standing against him. My own opinion is
that he could not have stopped his balls, and this
will be a criterion by which those who have seen
some of that gentleman's brilliant hits, may judge
of the extraordinary merit of this man's bowling.
He was considerably faster than Lambert, and so
superior in style and finish, that I can draw no
comparison between them. Lord Frederic Beau-
clerc has been heard to say that Harris's bowling
was one of the grandest things of the kind he had
ever seen ; but his lordship could not have known
him in his prime ; he never saw him play till after
he had had many fits of the gout and had become
slow and feeble.

To Harris's fine bowling I attribute the great improvement that was made in hitting, and, above all, in stopping; for it was utterly impossible to remain at the crease when the ball was tossed to a fine length; you were obliged to get in, or it would be about your hands or the handle of your bat, and every player knows where its next place would be.

JOHN NYREN.

Cycling Round Hambledon ◌ ◌

AN hour's easy run from Petersfield next day lands the pilgrim at the 'Bat and Ball' Inn [styled locally the 'Hut'], which has for all time been made famous by Nyren and the heroes of Hambledon. There are some who dispute this district being styled the cradle of cricket, but even if the game were born in Surrey or elsewhere, it was most decidedly cradled in Hampshire, the county that produced the first properly instituted club whose Eleven could hold its own against the Rest of England. I am never weary of exploring both the inside and the outside of this modest wayside hostelry, that appears so lonely and forlorn, the world forgetting, by the world forgot. Invariably I seat myself close to some ever-sighing Scotch firs and turn to gaze upon those sun-dried bricks, conjecturing how fascinating would be the story that they would tell if they could but speak. Then I endeavour to repeople Broad-Halfpenny Down, my thoughts busy with the happenings of more than a hundred and fifty years ago. Although the spell holds me, I am deliciously conscious of the salt-laden breeze and the small voices whispering through the wavering grass, musical whispers that careless ears would never heed or understand. It is always with difficulty that I drag myself away, although I know that there is more to enjoy.

W. R. WEIR.

THE CHARM OF CRICKET

Cricket ◡ ◡ ◡ ◡ ◡ ◡

AND so, my hibernating friend, you awake,
 Full fresh from out your winter hours of rest!
And they that wept to lose one single day
 Of your brave company, now laugh, now jest,
As you return. Your call is heard throughout
 The land, and English hearts and English eyes
Go out to you, and English hands stretch forth
 To show for you their love that never dies.

The Parish Match ◡ ◡ ◡ ◡

THERE is something strangely delightful in the
innocent spirit of party. To be one of a numerous
body, to be authorized to say *we*, to have a rightful
interest in triumph, or defeat, is gratifying at once to
social feeling and to personal pride. There was not
a ten-year-old urchin, or a septuagenary woman in
the parish, who did not feel an additional importance, a reflected consequence, in speaking of ' our
side.' An election interests in the same way ; but
that feeling is less pure. Money is there and hatred,
and politics, and lies. Oh, to be a voter, or a
voter's wife, comes nothing near the genuine and
hearty sympathy of belonging to a parish, breathing
the same air, looking on the same trees, listening

to the same nightingales! Talk of a patriotic elector! Give me a parochial patriot, a man who loves his parish! Even we, the female partisans may partake the common ardour. I am sure I did. I never, though tolerably eager and enthusiastic at all times, remember being in a more delicious state of excitation than on the eve of that battle. Our hopes waxed stronger and stronger. William Grey got forty notches off his own bat; and that brilliant hitter, Tom Coper, gained eight from two successive balls. As the evening advanced, too, we had encouragement of another sort. A spy, who had been dispatched to reconnoitre the enemy's quarters, returned from their practising-ground with a most consolatory report. 'Really,' said Charles Grover, our intelligencer—a fine old steady judge, one who had played well in his day— 'they are no better than so many old women. Any five of ours would beat their eleven.' This sent us to bed in high spirits.

Morning dawned less favourably. The sky promised a series of deluging showers, and kept its word, as English skies were wont to do on such occasions; and a lamentable message arrived at the head-quarters from our trusty comrade, Joel Brent. His master, a great farmer, had begun the hay-harvest that very morning, and Joel, being as eminent in one field as in another, could not be spared. Imagine Joel's plight! the most ardent of all our eleven! a knight held back from the tourney! a soldier from the battle! The poor swain was inconsolable. At last, one who is always ready to do a good-natured action, great or little, set forth to back his petition; and, by dint of appealing to the public spirit of our worthy neighbour, and the state of the barometer, talking alternately of the parish honour and thunder showers, of lost matches and sopped hay, he carried his point, and returned triumphantly with the delighted Joel.

At last we were all assembled, and marched down to H. common, the appointed ground, which, though in our domain according to the map, was the constant practising place of our opponents, and *terra incognita* to us. We found our adversaries on the ground, as we expected, for our various delays had hindered us from taking the field so early as we wished ; and, as soon as we had settled all preliminaries, the match began.

But, alas ! I have been so long settling my preliminaries that I have left myself no room for the detail of our victory, and must squeeze the account of our grand achievements into as little compass as Cowley, when he crammed the names of eleven of his mistresses into the narrow space of four eight-syllable lines.*

They began the warfare—these boastful men of B. And what think you, gentle reader, was the amount of their innings ? These challengers— the famous eleven—how many did they get ? Think ! Imagine ! Guess !—You cannot ?—Well ! they got twenty-two, or rather they got twenty ; for two of theirs were short notches, and would never have been allowed, only that, seeing what they were made of, we and our umpire were not particular. They should have had twenty more if they had chosen to claim them. Oh, how well we fielded ! and how well we bowled ! our good play

* The Chronicle, A Ballad.

had quite as much to do with their miserable failure as their bad. Samuel Long is a slow bowler, George Simmons a fast one, and the change from Long's lobbing to Simmon's fast balls passed them completely. Poor simpletons! they were always wrong, expecting the slow for the quick, and the quick for the slow. Well, we went in. And what were our innings? Guess again—guess! A hundred and sixty-nine! In spite of soaking showers, and wretched ground, where the ball would not run a yard, we headed them by a hundred and forty-seven; and then they gave in, as well they might. William Grey pressed them much to try another innings. 'There was so much chance,' as he cautiously observed, 'in cricket,' that advantageous as our position seemed, we might, very possibly, be overtaken. The B. men had better try. But they were beaten sulky, and would not move—to my great disappointment; I wanted to prolong the pleasure of success. What a glorious sensation it is to be for five hours together winning—winning—winning! always feeling what a whist-player feels when he takes up four honours, seven trumps! Who would think that a little bit of leather, and two pieces of wood, had such a delightful and delighting power.

Mary Russell Mitford.

A Poet on Cricket ∾ ∾ ∾ ∾

Lefroy once remarked that athletics had made him a poet. The simple fact is that he had an instinctive admiration for all that was beautiful and graceful in human form and movement into which he invariably tried to read a corresponding beauty of soul. Mr. Andrew Long complimented him as the first sonneteer on cricket.

In one of his letters Lefroy writes to a friend about cricket: ' My poetic soul gets an infusion of red blood whenever I am brought into contact with vigorous, energising humanity. There is something idyllic about the pastime. Given a bright day and a green sward, with a company of lithe young fellows scattered over it in picturesque attire—what could the artistic eye desire in addition ? " Earth has not anything to show more fair." . . . I play by proxy when I am able to watch the prowess of my luckier friends. *Floreat Cricket in œternum!*—It is something to be able to play cricket well. The whole edifice of the Christian virtues could be raised on a basis of good cricket.'

EDWARD CRACROFT LEFROY.

The Old Crocks in Session   ◡   ◡

Captain : It is strange that, apart from more or less prosaic records, cricket does not loom largely in our literature. As I say, this is strange, because cricket plays an important part in our national life. Of course, the subject comes up occasionally, as in *Tom Brown's Schooldays*, but it has not been treated as hunting has been for instance. There has been much verse of a kind written about it, going back from the time of the ' Surrey Poet ' to the Hambledon enthusiast who defiantly asked :

' What were Castor and Pollux to Nyren and Small.'

But the poetry is not of a high order.

Long-on : Coleridge seems to have known something of the game.

Wicket-keeper : Coleridge ! What on earth did he know about cricket ?

Long-on : Well, he evidently had a prophetic instinct about you as a wicket-keeper. Didn't he write of a man who ' stopped one of three ' ?

Wicket-keeper : Some people never have the courage to attempt to take the wicket.

Umpire : Over ! Over !

Long-on : Well, among our literary men at present Hesketh Pritchard is an excellent cricketer, and Conan Doyle is quite as good, while J. M, Barrie has written on the game and used to play occasionally for the Authors. Among other writers who take more or less interest in the game are Frankfort Moore, F. Meyrick-Jones, and A. E. W. Mason, and only the other day I turned up a very pretty little cricketing story called ' Kenyon's Innings,' by E. W. Hornung. Andrew Lang also loved the game and wrote about it. But I agree with the Captain that we are not rich in cricket literature. Books about particular tours, however well written, cannot have more than ephemeral interest. Disraeli does not mention the game in the *Amusements of the Learned*, and Emerson was evidently making a scornful reference to it when he said, ' Give an Englishmen a ball to play with and he is happy.'

Point : He did not forsee the baseball craze.

A. S. GARDINER.

The New Cricket Ground ∽ ∽ ∽

THE loveliness of Earth is still unspent :
Her beauties, singly known, combined are strange :
And with what fondness she doth freshly range
Her ancient gems for man's new ravishment !
On this soft dew-fed tree-girt sward of Kent
The cricket-god to-day is first enthroned,
The dun herd banished, and its pasture owned
By white-clad players and their snowy tent.
The field I knew before, the lads I knew,
And oft elsewhere have watched their pleasant
    game ;
But now an added lustre comes to view,
Familiar features look no more the same ;
The new-set picture gains another hue,
And sheds another glory on its frame.
            EDWARD CRACROFT LEFROY.

The Commentator ∽ ∽ ∽ ∽

THE throstle in the lilac,
   Not far beyond the Nets,
Upon a spray of purple
   His beak severely whets :
He hears the players calling,
   He wonders what they're at,
As thunder frequent Yorkers
   Against the stubborn bat.

And as the rank half-volley
   Its due quietus gets,
The bird begins to carol
   A greeting to the Nets :

C

Amazed at noisy kissing
   Of ball and wooden blade,
In rivalry he whistles
   A ballad unafraid.

The greatness of the uproar
   Benumbs him, and he lets
His pulsing bosom ponder
   The tumult in the Nets ;
But soon afresh, while warbling
   His comment on the game,
He puts all human songsters—
   Quite easily !—to   shame.

Thou Herrick in the lilac,
   The damp of evening wets
Upon our shoes the pipe-clay,
   And bids us leave the Nets ;
But come again to-morrow
   To mingle with our joy
The magic learnt in Eden
   When Time was but a boy !
                  NORMAN GALE.

Cricket !   The Most Kindly Nurse ◠

CRICKET is a very humanizing game. It appeals
to the emotions of local patriotism and pride. It is
eminently unselfish ; the love of it never leaves us,
and binds all the brethren together, whatever their
politics and rank may be. There is nothing like it
in the sports of mankind. Every one, however
young, can try himself at it, though excellence be
for the few, or perhaps not entirely for the few.
How much good cricket there is in the world ! . . .
    Cricket ought to be to English boys what Habeas

Corpus is to Englishmen, as Mr. Hughes says in *Tom Brown*.

At no ruinous expense, the village cricket might also be kept alive and improved ; for cricket is a liberal education in itself, and demands temper and justice and perseverance. There is more teaching in the playground than in school-rooms, and a lesson better worth learning very often. For there can be no good or enjoyable cricket without enthusiasm —without sentiment, one may almost say : a quality that enriches life and refines it ; gives it what life more and more is apt to lose—zest.

Though he who writes was ever a cricketing failure, he must acknowledge that no art has added so much to his pleasures as this English one, and that he has had happier hours at Lord's, or even on a rough country wicket, than at the Louvre or in the Uffizzi. If this be true of one, it is probably true of the many whose pleasures are scant, and can seldom come from what is called culture.

Cricket is simply the most catholic and diffused, the most innocent, kindly and manly of popular pleasures, while it has been the delight of statesmen and the relaxation of learning. There was an old Covenanting minister of the straitest sect, who had so high an opinion of curling that he said if he were to die in the afternoon, he could imagine no better way than curling of passing the morning. Surely we may say as much for cricket. Heaven (as the bishop said of the strawberry) might doubtless have devised a better diversion, but as certainly no better has been invented than that which grew up on the village greens of England.

ANDREW LANG.

Tom Hood on Cricket   ∽   ∽   ∽

'TWAS in the prime of summer-time,
   An evening calm and cool,
And four-and-twenty happy boys
   Came bounding out of school ;
There were some that ran, and some that leapt,
   Like troutlets in a pool.

Away they sped with gamesome minds,
   And souls untouched by sin ;
To a level mead they came, and there
   They drave the wickets in :
Pleasantly shone the setting sun
   Over the town of Lynn.

Childish Recollections   ∽   ∽   ∽

. . . IN scatter'd groups each favour'd haunt
   pursue,
Repeat old pastimes and discover new.
Flush'd with his rays, beneath the noontide sun,
In rival bands, between the wickets run,
Drive o'er the sward the ball with active force,
Or chase with nimble feet its rapid course.
          *   *   *   *   *
Friend of my heart, and foremost of the list
Of those with whom I lived supremely blest,
Oft have we drain'd the font of ancient lore ;
Though drinking deeply, thirsting still the more.
Yet, when confinement's lingering hour was done,
Our sports, our studies, and our souls were one :
Together we impell'd the flying ball,
Together waited in our tutor's hall ;

Together join'd in cricket's manly toil,
Or shared the produce of the river's spoil.

BYRON.[1]

The Village Ground ᘐ ᘐ ᘐ ᘐ

MY mind goes back to the old village cricket-field where I spent so many happy hours of my boyhood and youth. Its surroundings were delightful, for it was set in the midst of some of the finest country in England. From its green expanse we could see the hills covered with birch- and fir-trees, and along one side of the field the River Churnet gurgled and bubbled over its stony bed. How the birds sang on those bright spring mornings when we practised at the nets! What a symphony of glad colour and sound was all around us! . . .

And we were still there when the evening shadows began to fall and the swifts rose circling over the tree-tops, while from the farmhouse near by a thin column of smoke was rising straight into the air. Until at length, no longer able to watch the flight of the ball, we regretfully began to wend our way homeward through the gathering dusk. After supper to seek our beds and dream of ' hat-tricks,' and double centuries, which I am afraid remained merely dreams.   SAMUEL J. LOOKER.

Surrey Cricket In the Old Days ᘐ

' LET us now praise famous men, and our fathers that begot us.' Perhaps the writer of Ecclesiasticus will permit us to use his words with reference to

---

[1] In such verse as this Byron pays Pope the sincerest form of flattery.

the men who were famous for skill in the noblest
of all outdoor games.

It has been one of the privileges accorded to the
Vicar of Kennington, in past days, to witness, from
a window in the Vicarage, many a vast, good-humoured, happy crowd impartially cheering failures
and successes.

'What can be more enjoyable than a comfortable
seat on a fine day with a match to view and a pipe
to smoke ?' Such was one's reflection as one watched
one of the most curious effects one ever witnessed
on a certain Easter Monday.   Just as a ball was being
bowled apparently every one paused to give undivided attention to the result, and then—puff—
from 500 pipes there went up as many clouds of
smoke from the mass of spectators, just as if a
regiment had opened fire at a review. This
phenomenon certainly recurred throughout the
afternoon, and we could regularly time the moment
for the volley of smoke according as the company
paused to look, or relaxed their attention to keep
the pipes alight.   Long may the Oval continue to
afford good sport and the best of recreation to hard-
working South London !

BISHOP MONTGOMERY.

The Lamplight Match   ☞   ☞   ☞

THE question of light is always a difficult one for
umpires or captains to decide, but it may be of
nterest to recall the Surrey v. Yorkshire match
at the Oval more than thirty years ago. When
towards the end of the second day the prospect
of a finish seemed certain, the captains agreed to

play on until 6.45. As it was late in the month of August, the light at this hour can easily be imagined, but when the arranged time was reached eight runs were still required. The light had by then become very bad, but the captain of the home team, being allowed a free hand, elected to play to a finish, which resulted in a win for his side by two wickets shortly after seven o'clock. By this time the public lamps round the Oval were alight, and in consequence the match is always known as ' The Lamplight Match.'

JOHN SHUTER.

On Pavilion Critics ✌ ✌ ✌ ✌

THERE is no more justifiable occasion upon which a man may hold and express an opinion than during the progress of a cricket match ; but one is some-times inclined to wonder how long a large section of the public will be content to be gulled by the imposters who take a weird, if harmless, pleasure in posing as authorities. The fraud, however, is not intentional. The whole thing is so simple from the pavilion, and the fact that these savants lack experience in the field would seem to be in itself an incentive to them to talk with conviction and in blissful ignorance of their subject. Few of us probably realize how enormous is the number of pavilion critics who have never handled a bat, or who have merely done so as boys, much in the same way as they played with a rocking-horse or a toy train. Yet, with these passports, it is only fair to presume that they would hesitate to lay down the law concerning hunting or mechanical engineering. Naturally, they are men of a certain age, for in no community do we, without pretext, permit a boy to bounce, even if his own performances seem to entitle him to consideration. And, because this is so, the remedy is the more difficult to apply. The veneration with which we treat the possessor of the head that is streaked with silver is one of the most loveable traits in the national character ; but can we not call in the peers of these men to our assistance ? Will not some old Blue, when he hears one of these poor old things babbling from the front seat of the pavilion during a big match, go to him and gently lead him aside. Perhaps he might remind him of their early years spent together. Might he not say, ' You dear old fraud, come away and subdue your excitement. You know you never played the game in your life. At school you went in for butterflying and dominoes, and very good you were at both. Come away, old man, and have a whisky and soda, or a harmless cup of tea, and tell me about the roses you are growing in that wonderful garden of yours near Colchester, and how you have managed to get three first prizes already this summer.' And he might render a further service. Might he not whisper a word to the foolish reporter whom he has noticed hanging about his more than foolish old friend ? ' Come hither, you garnerer of stuff for an indiscriminating public ; let me plead with you not to take any notice of that old gentleman who is now quietly finishing his tea. When he has done he is going to talk to me about roses, and if you are interested come and join us. What ? Will I meanwhile say what I consider to be the peculiarity of Hayward's bowling to-day ? No, no ! I'm old, too, and out of date ; but I'll introduce you to that gentleman with the Forester ribbon on his hat, and at any rate if he has nothing to tell you on the subject he won't pretend he has.'

' But,' it may be urged, ' you can't expect to get a crowd of experts in a pavilion ; and men will talk about things which interest them.' Undoubtedly this is so, but the pavilion critics insist on their remarks being considered in the light of judgments rather than as mere conversation or harmless chatter ; and surely they should not feel annoyed when they explain in detail exactly when Lord Hawke should have changed the bowling or how Abel should have pulled the long-hop, if one suddenly remembers that one has a train to catch. On the other hand, they support cricket, and for that they merit thanks. They pay their subscriptions and write their names on the benefit lists of the leading professionals ; and if their advocacy does not cause others to do the same it is not their fault. It is certainly unfortunate that a cricket-match should lure the foolish traits in our characters out of their concealment ; but perhaps we may excuse ourselves under the plea of zeal and enthusiasm—and after all, when zeal and enthusiasm wane, we may make up our minds that we are going down the hill. ' Every club has its old man of cricket,' said a player of some note, who has listened more indulgently than his friend to the wanderings of a particularly fierce type of a pavilion cricketer. ' Possibly,' was the curt reply, ' but in this club we have about a hundred and fifty of him.' CAPTAIN PHILIP TREVOR.

The Greatest Outdoor Game

CRICKET is the greatest outdoor game in the world. He who plays it in the right spirit learns endurance, is taught to keep his temper under trying circumstances, gives up his own selfish interests for the sake of the general good, and practises himself in undergoing a hard day's work, when eye and hand and foot are hard put to it, to overcome rivals in healthy combat. And if a man is called to be captain of an eleven he learns in his youth how to manage men, to be quick in resolution, warm in commendation, a judge of character, and a tower of strength in the moment of discouragement. Need we add a word more to prove that cricket must even be the great English game? It is more than a game : it is an education. I am ready to own that had it not been for a long apprenticeship to this sport I should not have learnt some of the most priceless lessons of life—lessons which are indispensable for all, however high they may rise in Church or State. Some learn them in the study, some in the tented field. Since success in after life depends upon *character*, English gentlemen must win their character by nobleness displayed in all their pursuits. Long may cricket continue to be the nursery for healthful, unselfish, openhanded, and generous-hearted young men.

BISHOP MONTGOMERY.

A Boy's Prayer in 1897

' AND, please God,' Johnny was heard by his mother to whisper, by way of postscript to his evening prayer, ' please make me play like Jessop.'

Cricket and Cupid ◇ ◇ ◇ ◇

Sнe understands the game no more
　　Than savages the sun's eclipse ;
For all she knows the bowler throws,
　　And Square-Leg stands among the Slips :
And when in somersaults a stump
　　Denotes a victim of the game,
Her lovely throat begets a lump,
　　Her cheeks with indignation flame.

　　　　*　　*　　*　　*　　*

Sweet are her little cries, and sweet
　　The puzzled look her forehead wears ;
For all she knows the Umpire goes
　　Away to Leg to say his prayers.
And yet, so velvety her eyes,
　　I even find a charm in this,
And think, How foolish to be wise
　　When Ada's ignorance is bliss !

NORMAN GALE.

The Curate ◇ ◇ ◇ ◇ ◇

A Christian meek, a scholar fine,
　　Our Curate, enemy of strife,
Who told us of the love divine,
　　And showed it in his daily life ;
Our Curate, teacher in the school,
　　Friend of the poor, the rich man's guide,
Gentle in talk, yet firm in rule,
　　And a good *Cricketer* beside.
A man whom all the parish lov'd
So winning in his words and ways.

The Ruling Passion

A HALF-WITTED fellow, who had been made drunk by an unprincipled companion, fell into a ditch on going from the field towards home. 'Let me help you up, old man,' said one, compassionating his helpless condition. 'Are you a cricketer?' hiccuped the inebriate, ''cos no man shall ever help me who is not a good cricketer.'

AN OLD CRICKETER.

The Forerunners

BESIDE the pillar-box a girl
  Sells daffodils in golden bunches,
And with an apron full of Spring
  Stays men a moment from their lunches :
Some fill their hands for love of bloom,
  To others Cupid hints a reason ;
But as for me, I buy because
  The flowers suggest the Cricket season !

Although I trouble not to seek
  A maiden proud to wear my favour,
Right glad am I to change my pence
  For blooms, and smell their wholesome savour ;
For as I carry blossoms home—
  Sisters of gold with golden sisters—
My heart is thumping at the thought
  Of pads and bails and slow leg-twisters.

My only sweetheart is a bag—
  A faithful girl of dark brown leather,
Who's travelled many a mile with me
  In half a hundred sorts of weather !

Once more to clasp your friendly hand,
  To tramp along by Hope attended,
Dreaming of glances, drives, and cuts,
  My Dear Old Girl, how truly splendid!

NORMAN GALE.

Cricket on the Hearth ⌣   ⌣   ⌣

How great a game to fill July,
    May, June, and August with delights,
      Yet in the frost
      Be never lost,
  But stir the blood on nipping nights!
For Cricket is played again, again,
    At freezing-time in Hull or Bath;
When Summer's done the game's not gone—
  There's Cricket on the Hearth!

NORMAN GALE.

Miss Wicket *   ⌣   ⌣   ⌣   ⌣

(On her Picture)

OF your Chlöes you poets may sing,
  And you lovers of Delia may sigh,
All the hills with 'Orynthia!' may ring,
  An' you list for your Capulet die,
Carve your Rosalind's name in the thicket,
  With your Thisbe converse through the wall;
But I'll sing the due praise of Miss Wicket,
  Of Miss Wicket, the fairest of all.

* By E. B. V. Christian, from *At the Sign of the Wicket,* by permission of the Author.

Amaryllis may sport in the shade,
  Roxalana hold sway o'er the stage,

And the ghost of poor Slender, unlaid,
  May still hopelessly sigh for Anne Page ;
Gloriana the Court may command,
  And Dorinda may rule in the Mall ;
But of all the fair dames in the land,
  Mistress Wicket's the fairest of all.

By the groves where your Phillida dreams,
  By the woods where your Amoret strays,
By the path where beneath the moon's beams
  You make sonnets in Cynthia's praise,
You may sue, and may sigh, and may plead ;
  Yet your fortune to mine is but small
While I woo on a fair level mead
  Mistress Wicket, the fairest of all.

To you rakes I will faro resign,
  To you curates your sober Pope Joan ;
But the joys of great cricket be mine
  Till the summer is over and flown.
You may play at your ombre or piquet,
  I will throw, not the dice, but the ball,
And I'll sing the due praise of Miss Wicket,
  Of Miss Wicket, the fairest of all.
                              E. B. V. CHRISTIAN.

Traddles : The Autocrat of the Cricket Field

No, this is not about Grace. It is about Traddles.
Traddles has only lately brought his cricket season
to an end. From the statement that he recently

finished the season it will be gathered that Traddles
is an enthusiast at cricket. He is. When other
players are thinking of putting their bats away for
the winter, he is as keen as ever, showing no sign
of the exhaustion which a long season is supposed
to produce, and determined (with the reluctant
assistance of his brothers and sisters) to go on
pitching the wicket until rain finally puts the game
out of the question. Despite his enthusiasm, however, he has not yet attained first-class county
form. As a matter of fact, he is in his fifth year.

We have to play our cricket under somewhat
serious disadvantages. Our ground is a plot of grass
at the back of the house, and, not only are the
boundaries inconveniently narrow—rendering a
toilsome journey over the fences a frequent necessity—but some of the best strokes are spoiled by
the contiguity of fruit-trees. However, the conditions are quite good enough for Traddles, and
whenever the opportunity arises he pounces upon
me and drags me off to the scene of operations.
Sometimes we put up the stumps ; occasionally a
wine case serves in their place. It is quite a matter
of indifference to him. . . .

Our procedure is generally something like this :
I take up my position, as bowler, at a spot indicated
by Traddles, and regarded by him as the most
convenient for his own purposes. He holds the
bat, with the forefinger of his right hand down the
blade and his left hand hopelessly out of place. . . .
A smile of contentment passes over the curl-framed
face of Traddles, and we make a start. I send the
ball down slowly, and directly the young rascal
catches sight of it he throws all the principles of

the game to the winds, and prepares for a mighty slog.   If he misses the ball his legs are conveniently in the way, so that the chances of bowling him are rather unfairly reduced.

Nor is it easy to run him out.   It is quite true he starts for the smallest hit, but, as he decides when his run is completed, and that is always just before the wicket is put down, he incurs no risks. Occasionally, he astonishes himself so thoroughly by a particularly slashing hit that, in following the course of the ball in silent admiration, he forgets to run.   When he recovers from his surprise, however, and appreciates the situation, he calmly adds two or three to his total.   We have never yet unravelled the mysteries of his method of reckoning, but there can be no doubt about its effectiveness, for his score rises with a rapidity that would excite the envy of even Jessop. . . .

Perhaps you catch Traddles out.   He drops the bat between his knees, claps his hands in a most generous fashion, calls out, ' well catched, sir,' and coolly takes up his position to play the ball again. Or, by a lucky chance, you clean bowl him.   Even then he is not out.   He emphatically decides that it was a trial ball, and that he is entitled to continue his innings. . . .

All things, however, must come to an end at some time, and even Traddles's innings has eventually to be closed.   Now and then he retires with a good grace, but occasionally he protests indignantly against the injustice that is being done when he is requested to leave after having been caught or bowled five or six times.   No, it is not an easy thing to dispose of Traddles as a batsman.

Like many other cricketers, he has a soul above fielding, and persistently declines to take an active interest in it. He spends the greater part of the time between his innings in the consumption of sweets and apples, but sometimes we seduce him from these delights of childhood, as being beneath the dignity of a cricketer, and it is the pleasantest part of our game to see him pursuing the ball—his little slippered feet toiling one over the other, and his curly head wagging from side to side. I am doubtful whether Traddles will ever become a batsman. He is too impetuous, and his defence is deplorably weak. On the other hand, he possesses a qualification which I have observed distinguishes most eminent cricketers, and that is a ready resource in discovering excuses for his own failure. In any case, I am quite sure that, whatever the future may have in store for me, it can bring no greater delight than I experience in bowling to Traddles.

A. S. GARDINER.

Cricket—the Teacher ∽ ∽ ∽

WE must guard against all extreme statements as to what cricket is. It certainly is not an end in itself. Even all-round success in it is not an end in itself; still less is success in some one branch only. . . .

Cricket is not merely a muscle-maker, a sort of gymnastic drill which scarcely trains the nerves at all. To run out to a ball, to stand up to a fast bowler and not draw away the right foot, to field a hard drive, this means nerve. Nor is Cricket merely a physical health-maker or disease-palliator.

To have practised and played it properly is quite impossible without some mental and moral exercise and health as well ; it is a social game of the best kind—it is a great bond of union. Far above brainless frivolity, farther above mere recreation, it can be a preparation for the whole of life, even for business life ; for it can teach co-operation, specialization, patience, observation, promptness, full extension, use of great weight and power without loss of poise. It can be valuable for all life, which mere muscle-straining without nerve-training, mere disease, avoidance, mere amusement, cannot possibly be.

E. F. Benson and E. H. Miles.

Next, Please !

What could be more delightful than the story of Morley, the Notts bowler, who always went in last, and was so bad a bat that when he came down the pavilion steps the old horse used instinctively to walk over and place itself between the shafts of the roller ? And there is one told of Barlow, who played local cricket for a railway team and whom the porters had been trying to get out for three weeks. He was a terrible stonewaller, and one would like to know how many runs he had made in the time.

P. F. Warner.

CRICKET IN THE PAST

An Heroic Poem [1]   ⌒   ⌒   ⌒   ⌒

HAIL Cricket ! glorious, manly, British Game !
First of all sports ! be first alike in fame !
To my fir'd Soul thy busy transports bring,
That I may feel thy Raptures, while I sing !
O thou, sublime Inspirer of my Song !
What matchless trophies to thy worth belong !
Look round the earth, inclin'd to mirth, and see
What daring sport can claim the prize from *thee* !

Not puny Billiards, where, with sluggish pace,
The dull ball trails before the foolish face,
Where nothing can your languid spirits move,
Save when the Marker bellows out, Six love !
Nor yet that happier Game, where the smooth Bowl,
In circling mazes, wanders to the goal ;
Not Tennis self, thy sister sport, can charm,
Or with thy fierce delights our bosoms warm.
For, to small space confined, ev'n she must yield
To nobler Cricket, the disputed field.

O parent Britain ! minion of renown !
Whose far-extended fame all nations own ;
Nurs'd on thy plains, first Cricket learnt to please,
And taught thy sons to slight inglorious ease ;

[1] Published in 1744.

37

And see where busy Counties strive for fame,
Each greatly potent at this mighty game !
Fierce Kent, ambitious of the first applause,
Against the world combin'd, asserts her cause ;
Gay Sussex sometimes triumphs o'er the field,
And fruitful Surrey cannot brook to yield.
While London, Queen of Cities ! proudly vies,
And often grasps the well-disputed prize.
Thus while Greece triumph'd o'er the barb'rous
    earth,
Seven cities struggl'd which gave Homer birth.[1]

                   JOHN LOVE.

' *When was Cricket invented ?* ' ∽   ∽

THE earliest mention of cricket-playing in England
is in the poetic writings of Joseph of Exeter, A.D.
1180, who sings, in the old style :

> ' The youths at cricks did play
>   Throughout the merry day.'

He then proceeds to describe the game, which is
evidently the same as our cricket. He talks of
the *two* sticks with a third across the top ; of one
knight throwing the ball at these sticks, and of
another trying to prevent the ball hitting them,
while a third player, a serf, stops the ball when it

---

[1] *Author's Note.*—Our author has nothing to plead in
favour of this simile, but poetic practice. He con-
fesses it is very little to the purpose ; but then the absolute necessity of introducing similies somewhere, the
flavour they give to a poem, and the prodigious esteem
they are in at present, were arguments which his modesty
was obliged to give way to.

passes the sticks. We have, however, an earlier record than this, of its being played in Italy by Eustatius Cartonius, a monk of the eighth century. He says it was much played at Florence, the Cardinals even being present to witness the sport. It is described by him much in the same manner as by Joseph of Exeter. Chaucer mentions cricket in his *Canterbury Tales*.

' *A Crooked Stick* '

THE word CRICKET is related to *cric* or *cryc* (Saxon), crooked stick. In the wardrobe account of Edward I for 1300, there occurs an entry of a payment for a *creagh*, which is the earliest allusion to the game by a term analogous to the modern word cricket, which is believed to be a diminutive suggesting a short staff or club.

The Plantagenet kings disapproved of all games as tending to interfere with the practice of archery, and in 1447–8 a particularly severe edict was issued by Edward IV, by which it was proposed to imprison for three years anyone who allowed the game on his premises, and to fine him £20 besides, while the players were liable to a fine of £10, two years' imprisonment, and the tools were to be burnt. In the infancy of the game there were no stumps, a large hole serving as a wicket. In the Chronicles of England is a representation of two male figures playing a game with a bat and ball, and in the Romance of Good King Alexander appears a drawing of a batsman and bowler and four fielders, all monks. Both these are of the thirteenth century, and no stumps were shown in either.

Some Patrons of Cricket ∽ ∽ ∽

THOUGH we may regret that the great game was at one-time not as pure from gambling as it is now, still we may well bestow an ample measure of honour on those old-time enthusiasts who supported it so valiantly, and who are the shadowy figures that show themselves momentarily through the mists of centuries ? First then, I think, our hats off to John Derrick, Coroner of Surrey, who in 1598 bore witness that fifty years before he had played ' crickett and other places ' on a certain waste at Guildford ; and then, a century later, to Wright and Valyer, those worthies of Marden, in the Weald of Kent, who welcomed every one who did ' delight in cricket.' The mists roll up very thick in the next fifty years, and it is not until 1708 that we find Thomas Minter, of Canterbury, recording in his diary that ' We beat Ash Street at Crickets.' Good old Tom Minter, of Canterbury, worthy ancestor of a noted East Kent family of yeomen and farmers, we would have welcomed a longer account of that match than your brief record.

But what of the patrons ? Pride of place in the long column of those who have pushed the game along through evil as well as good report, must be given to ' Edward Stead, or Stede, Esq., of Maidstone.' This was undoubtedly Mr. Edwyn Stede, of Stede Hill, Harrietsham, near Maidstone. After 180 years the leader of the Kentish XI again comes from that parish. Though Mr. Stede's name constantly appears after 1726, the first mention of him is brought about by a curious incident. His side had the better of a match against Chingford

but the Chingford men refused to fight to a finish ;
so Mr. Stede appealed to the law, but Chief Justice
Pratt—oh, wise old judge—' referred the said
cause back to Dartford Heath, to be played on where
they left off, and a rule of Court was made accordingly.' That experience doubtless showed the law-
makers of cricket the wisdom of relying on the
Laws of Cricket to decide their disputes, for I think
cricket has been remarkably free from dispute in the
Courts of Law.

Mr. Stede was evidently at that date the leader of
the Kent XI, who are recorded as playing out and
home matches with ' the Londoners ' in 1719 ; and
in 1729 they were strong enough to play an XI
selected from Sussex, Surrey and Hampshire. The
Duke of Richmond and Sir William Gage were the
patrons in Sussex.

A struggling and unimportant pastime attracted
the attention of Royalty, in the person of Frederick
Prince of Wales, who was by no means the
insignificant person the Jacobite lampooners tried
to make him out to be. Evidently there must
have been sterling merit in the game even then for
a Prince, who had been brought up abroad and had
perhaps never seen a game of cricket until he was
grown up and had taken up his residence in England,
to give his patronage to it with such zeal and
practical enthusiasm. The patronage of his Royal
Highness must have been of immense assistance to
those still earlier patrons of the game, who doubtless
had a hard struggle to induce the public to support
it.

LORD HARRIS.

Early References to the Game ∽ ∽

THE word 'cricket' appears in the following work, being about the first time mentioned in any dictionary. *A Worlde of Wordes, or most copious and exact dictionarie in Italian and English, collected by J. Florio.* Printed in London 1598.

'*Sgrillare*, to make a noise as a cricket, to play cricket-a-wicket, and be merry.'

In a dictionary of French and English by Randle Cotgrave, 1611, which seems to be the first dictionary giving the word 'cricket,' the following appears : '*Crosse*, f.—a crosier, or Bishop's staffe ; also a cricket staff ; or the crooked staffe ; wherewith boys play at cricket. *Crosser*—to play at cricket.'

*　　*　　*　　*　　*

In the *Life of Thomas Wilson*, Minister of Maidstone, published anonymously in 1672, page 40, the following is mentioned : ' Maidstone was formerly a very profane town, inasmuch that I have seen morrice-dancing, cudgle-playing, stool-ball, crickets, and many other sports openly and publickly indulged on the Lord's Day.'

*　　*　　*　　*　　*

In *Voyages and Travels of the Ambassadors*, by John Davies, 1662, page 297, the following appears : ' They play there also a certain game which the Persians call Kuitskaukan, which is a kind of mall or cricket.'

*　　*　　*　　*　　*

In the *Works of Rabelais*, 1653, translated by Sir Thomas Urchard (Urquhardt), vol. I, page 61, is the following reference : The games of Gargantua.

There he played cricket. This being one of the games mentioned.

*   *   *   *   *

The Diary of Henry Teonge.—' On May 6, 1676, this morning early (as the custom is all the summer long) at least forty of the English, with his worship the Consull, rode out of the city about four miles to the Greene Platt, a fine valley by the river syde, to recreate themselves, where a princely tent was pitched ; and we had several pastimes and sports, as duck-hunting, fishing, shooting, hand-ball, *krickett*, scrofilo ; and then a noble dinner brought thither, with greate plenty of all sorts of wines, and lemonade, and at six we returned home in good order, but soundly tired and weary.'

*   *   *   *   *

From *The Weekly Journal or Saturday's Post*, 1720.—' July 16 : Last week was played a match in White-Conduit-Fields by Islington ; between 11 Londoners on one side, and 11 men of Kent on the other side, for 5s. a head ; at which time, being in eager pursuit of the game, the Kentish men having the wickets, two Londoners striving with expedition to gain the ball, met each other with that fierceness, that hitting their heads together they both fell backwards without stirring hand or foot, and lay deprived of sense for a considerable time, and 'tis not yet known (at that time) whether they will recover. The Kentish men were beat.'

*   *   *   *   *

' On Monday, July 26, 1731, a great cricket match was play'd on Chelsea Common, between 11 of London, and the like number of Brompton, for £5 a-head, which was won by great odds by the former.

As soon as the match was over a quarrell happened between a Londoner and a Brompton gentleman, occasioned by the latter's tearing the former's ruffles from off his shirt, swearing he had no property to them, when several engaged on both sides for nearly half an hour, and most of the Brompton gentlemen were forced to fly for quarters, and some retired home with black eyes, and broken heads, much to the satisfaction of the opposite side.'

* * * * *

London Magazine, 1744, page 307.—'Monday, June 18, was played in the Artillery Ground the greatest Cricket-Match ever known, the County of Kent played against All England, which was won by the former. There were present their Royal Highnesses the Prince of Wales and Duke of Cumberland, the Duke of Richmond, Admiral Vernon, and many other persons of distinction.'

* * * * *

1747.—'This day, July 13, will be played in the Artillery Ground, the match of cricket so long expected, between the women of Charlton, in Sussex, against the women of Westdean, and Chilgrove, in the same county. It is hoped, that the paying sixpence of admission to this match will not be taken amis, the charges thereof amounting to upwards of four score pounds. Wickets pitched at 2 o'clock.'

* * * * *

In playing the above match, the company broke in, so that it was impossible for the game to be played out ; and some of them being very much frightened, and others hurt, it could not be finished till this morning (July 14) when at 9 o'clock they will start to finish the same, hoping the company will be so kind as to indulge them in not walking within the ring, which will not only be a great pleasure to them, but a general satisfaction to the whole. All ladies and gentlemen who have paid to see this match on Monday, shall have the liberty of the ground to see it finished, without any other charge. And in the afternoon they will play a second match in the same place, several large sums being depending. The women of the Hills of Sussex will be in orange-coloured ribbons, and those of the Dales, in blue ; wickets to be pitched at 1 o'clock, and begin at 2.'

*　　*　　*　　*　　*

'1747, July 16, will be played a game of cricket in Eastwell Park, between Milton and New Romney, for half a guinea a man, no dogs to be allowed in the Park.

'N.B.—There will be a good ordinary provided at Robt. Cheeseman's, at the Flying Horse, at Boughton Lees, to be on the table at 12 o'clock.'

*　　*　　*　　*　　*

1752, June 28.—'This is to give notice to all gentlemen cricketers. That the long depending match is to be played at Lowlayton, between the gentlemen of Hackney, and the gentlemen of Layton and Walthamstow, on Coppey Down, near the Bowling Green, July 29, for £50.'

*　　*　　*　　*　　*

1771, May 13.—'This is to give notice to all gentlemen cricket-players, and others, that there be 11 good hats of 5s. value, each, to be played for at Cricket, on Tunworth Down, on Whitmonday, for the two sides that appear on the Down by 10 o'clock in the morning, each man to pay 2s. 6d.

The wickets to be pitched at 1 o'clock. A hat will be given to the Umpire on the winning side.

'If the game should not be played out that night, it shall be decided when the parties think proper, as there is no money to be returned. Likewise a good hat to be bowled for, and a set of ribbons to be danced for, each person that dances to put in a sixpence.'

At their very humble servant's,
RICHARD MOTT (Reading).

*   *   *   *   *

'On Tuesday last, June 9, 1783, a match of cricket was played on Old Field, near Maidenhead, by 11 gentlemen by the name of Boult, all near relations, and the parish of Bray, which was decided in favour of the former, by a majority of 26 notches. The Umpire and Scorer were also named Boult, and nearly related to the 11.'

*   *   *   *   *

1784.—'On Monday, July 19, the most manly of all exercises, the game of cricket, was played near Harwich, for the second time, between the gentlemen of Landguard-Fort and Colness Hundred, against 11 of the Harwich club, which was decided in favour of the latter by 109 notches. The politeness of the former in giving the Harwich 11 the opportunity of going in first, and the generous return they made in beating the stump down before they were all out, to give the others time to decide the contest, gave more than general satisfaction to every spectator.'

*   *   *   *   *

1793.—'On July 8, a match of Cricket was played at Witney, in the county of Oxford, the married men against the bachelors, for a considerable sum, which terminated in favour of the latter. The amazing skill, and dexterity, agility, displayed by these competitors for the reward of the winged goddess, both pleased and astonished the polite company assembled on this occasion. As soon as the match was decided, the conquerors. and the conquered adjourned to the Red Lion Inn, where they sat down to an elegant repast, concluding the day in friendship and glee.'

The Stumps

IN course of time—but when is not known now— one stump was introduced, and about 1700 a second added. These stumps were each 12 inches high by 24 wide, and a piece of wood—the forerunner of the bails—was laid along the top of them. In 1702 the stumps were 22 inches high by 6 wide. Terrible injuries to the hands were often occasioned in these days of two stumps by the rule which made it necessary to run a man out by popping the ball in a hole between the two stumps, while the batsman had to place his bat in the same hole, for the batsman, in his desperate eagerness to get in, would often drive his bat on to the hands which had anticipated him by the fraction of a second. The introduction of a third stump in 1775 terminated this practice, and was one great step in the civilization of the game. The name popping-crease, within which the batsman has now to ground his bat, is a survival from this practice. In 1798 the stumps were altered to 24 inches high and 7 wide, and in 1817 to 27 inches high and 8 wide, at which they remain.

Prior to 1700, 18 inches high—1 stump
About 1700, 12 inches high, 24 wide—2 stumps
Prior to 1702, 22 ,, ,, 6 ,, 2 ,,
3rd stump added 1775, 22 ,, ,, 6 ,, 3 ,,
1798, 24 ,, ,, 7 ,, 3 ,,
1814, 26 ,, ,, 8 ,, 3 ,,
1817, 27 ,, ,, 8 ,, 3 ,,

The Kentish Cricketers : in 1773

Kent, who is famed for men of skill,
Whom Nature formed to climb the hill,
Descend the vale with rapid flight,
And shine heroic men of might,
Agreed, a *Cricket Match* to play
With *Surrey* men, as famed as they.

In July last, at Bishopsborne,
Before the golden shocks of corn
Were rear'd by the laborious hind,
To ease the anxious farmer's mind,
The matchless cricketers were seen
In milk-white vestments tread the green ;
Where the smooth grass was laid compleat
Before Sir Horace Mann's Retreat ;
When the sweet lawn, with shady trees
Encompass'd round—sensation's please !
The rural prospect of the grove,
Nature so kindly made for love—
The towering hill, and neighb'ring vale,
The gliding stream of the canal :
But view the scene ! description's faint ;
My pen its beauties cannot paint.

From distant Counties many came,
To see the Herculean game ;
Nobles, Squires, Captain's view ;
Physicians, Lawyers, Rectors too,
Flying in haste, the sport to see,
Which *Rustics* call, their *Jubilee.*

Lumpey [1] appears, whose steady eye,
And nervous arm makes wickets fly,
Calls for the Kentish men to play,
For Miller, Simmons, Louch, and May.

First Miller came, who stands confest
Of England's Cricketers the best ;
With nervous hand, and manly strength,
He'll pitch a ball its proper length ;
Will run, stop, throw, and catch, to please,
And play the skilful game with ease.

His Grace the Duke of Dorset came,
The next enroll'd in skilful fame,
Equall'd by few, he plays with glee,
Nor peevish seeks for victory.
His Grace for bowling, cannot yield
To none but Lumpey in the field ;
And for unlike the *Modern* way,
Of blocking every ball at play,
He firmly stands with bat upright,
And strikes with athletic might,
Sends forth the ball across the mead,
And scores six notches for the deed.

[1] *Author's Note.*—Stevens, *alias* Lumpey, a Surrey cricketer, esteem'd the best bowler in England.

The active Simmons ne'er will yield
To man, whene'er he skims the field;
Close to the wicket now he stands,
With piercing eyes, and anxious hands,
Eager to catch the wish'd-for prize,
And heave victorious to the skies:
View him now swiftly fly the mead
O'ertake the rapid ball with speed,
And instantaneous throw the same
So just, to gain immortal fame;
All, all, must own, who saw the feat—
Of *Field's-men*, he's the most compleat.

Davis, who loves a game of cricket,
(And shines whene'er he keeps the wicket)
The next appears—with manly mien
He firmly treads the slipp'ry green.

     *   *   *   *   *

And now the Umpires take their stand,
To aid decision's timid hand,
And underneath the shady tree
The Scorer's fixed the runs to see.

     *   *   *   *   *

How, great the pleasure! to enjoy
Amusements which can never cloy;
View but the drunkard as he reels,
And ask next morning what he feels:
He'll tell you, pain succeeds the pleasure,
As misers when they lose their treasure.
The gambler too, with anxious care,
Can seek the rich illit'rate heir:
Rob him of all his golden pelf—
Spend it!—and then destroy himself.

Ye manly, skilful Sons of Kent,
Who seek diversions and content ;
Say ! What delight can fill the breast,
Where innocency lives confest ?
Your noble exercise will stand
The first amusement in the land,
While *Kentish Cricketers*, of fame,
Immortalize their conquering name.

JOHN BURNBY.[1]

---

[1] The author of this energetic poem was an Attorney-at-Law in Canterbury. He was a fierce partisan of his native county and an enthusiastic sportsman. I have come across references to his zeal in contemporary records.

E

GIANTS OF THE PAST

Old Cricketers and Hard Knocks ✐

' THE fingers of an old cricketer, so shattered, so indented, so contorted, so venerable ! are enough to bring tears of envy and emulation from any eye— we are acquainted with such a pair of hands ; if hands they may be called, that shape have none ! But wounds did not deter those heroic, unprotected men. ' We never thought of knocks,' said Beld-ham to Mr. Pycroft in 1837.

WILLIAM MITFORD.

Old John Bowyer of Mitcham ✐ ✐

DIRECTLY the spring comes on, old John is to be seen on the cricket ground, sometimes as umpire in a village match—for with the exception of a trifling defeat of sight and hearing, his knowledge of the game and his intellects are as good as ever— sometimes as a spectator, sitting in a chair under one of the trees, with his accustomed pipe in his mouth, and a glass of ale by his side.

Anyone can imagine what a delight it must have been to me in the dead of winter, when the cricket spark is extinguished in the minds of most men (except amiable lunatics like myself) to get old John up to my house, and place him in an easy-chair in front of the fire, give him his pipe, and his glass of beer—in the drinking whereof he is very moderate—and listen to his account of cricket, played sixty years ago ; and especially is it a delight when that account comes from a man who played against six of the old Hambledon Club, viz., W. Beldham, Walker, Lambert (the little farmer), Fennex, Wells, and Robinson. He played also in six matches of B's v. England, and his career opened in the days of Mr. E. H. Budd, Mr. W. Ward, Mr. Assheton Smith, Lord Frederick Beauclerk, Mr. George Osbaldeston, and others of their time, and continued down to 1838.

An hour or two with old John is like talking to a man from the dead, and his account of cricketers of his time exactly tallies with what I frequently heard from the late Mr. William Ward five and twenty years ago and upwards.

The old man says that the player's dress was generally nankeen breeches, silk stockings (which were often provided by noblemen or gentlemen who supported the game) with a pair of socks pulled on over them, and rolled over the ankle, laced boots, with sparrowbills (small rough nails), white shirts, and hats ; gentlemen wore white hats.

The bats used by the players were much superior to those specimens of old bats which are occasionally now found in country villages ; but though they were heavier and thicker than those now in use, the weight and balance were carefully considered.

The bowling was mostly of a good pace, and some of it so fast as to require two long-stops.

The field were placed differently to our present

system. Leg-hitting was almost unknown in first-rate matches, owing to the straightness of the bowling. If the bowling was middle-paced and the bowler was apt to over-pitch, a field was placed square with the wicket and called ' hip,' in the place where square-leg stands now, on the look-out for a catch from a full pitch to the body.

The long-fields, three in number, one being behind the bowler, stood very deep ; middle on and middle off stood about twelve or fifteen yards off at right angles with the wickets ; long-leg and long-slip stood deep and played very fine, and were expected to cover the long-stop in case of a bye, and point would sometimes stand almost close enough to take the ball off the bat.

' It was no joke,' said the old man, ' to play without pads and gloves on a bumpy down against quick bowling. We had first to look after our wickets, for many men would bowl (which word he pronounces as " owl ") thirty-nine balls out of forty straight to the wicket ; and then you must remember that there were as many kinds of under-hand bowling as there are now of round. One man would turn his wrist with his thumb right out ; another would do precisely the reverse. One would run with his right hand up in the air and bring it down with a swing, like the fan of a wind-mill ; and another—Lambert, the little farmer, for instance—would send them in with his hand almost on the ground, and yet pitch a good length.'

' Then, sir, you must remember the rough ground which made the long hops so difficult. First you had to mind the shooter, and if the ball pitched short and rose she would be on your knuckles, and if you played her back, point had a rare chance of taking her almost off the bat, if she popped up.

'We used to get our runs mostly by draws, little tips in the slips, and hard driving on or off. If the ground was hard and the ball not likely to shoot, every over-pitched ball was hit right away—a ball which might or might not take the inner stump, if only half-wicket high, would be met with a straight bat, with the pad slanted a little from the wicket and drawn behind, or if to the off, dropped in the slips ; and with a good partner backing up either of those hits would generally be worth one run— as the watches were placed deep—and if not within the fieldsman's reach they might be worth four or five ; for, remember, sir, we played mostly on large unenclosed grounds.'

Bowyer claims Beldham of the old Hambledon Club as the best all-round player he ever saw in the days of underhand. He could do anything in the field or with the bat. But of all the old Hambledon men he says the same, ' They were backbone players, ready to go till they dropped, and never sick or sorry in a match.'

There is one thing on his mind as regards Fennex, which is, that forty-eight years ago when Mitcham played Blackheath, Fennex, who played for the latter, backed his side for a glass of brandy and water, and, says old John, ' *he has never paid me to this day.*' FREDERICK GALE.

Tom Walker's Stonewalling

TOM WALKER'S stonewalling seems to have been of an aggravated—not to say aggravating—order.

Nyren tells of Lord Frederick Beauclerk bowling to him an over, every ball of which ' he dropped down just before his bat.' The historian adds : ' Off went his lordship's white hat—dash upon the ground (his constant action when disappointed)— calling him at the same time " a confounded old beast." ' Tom merely remarked : ' I doant care what ee zays.' Lord Frederick must have been, from his peppery nature, an interesting figure in the cricket field.

' *Silver Billy* '

WILLIAM BELDHAM was a wonderful cricketer. He was born near Farnham in 1766, but lived the greater part of his life near Tilford. He was for many years thought to be the best batsman in England, and was called ' a most venomous hitter.' He played in all the great matches for thirty-five years, which is itself a remarkable performance, for begin your first-class matches at what age you will, thirty-five years take most men into the stiff and heavy stage of life. Fennex, whose name occurs in so many ' England ' matches, spoke more highly of Beldham than of any cricketer of his day. He was extraordinarily quick, and sometimes was able to turn round and hit G. Brown's bowling towards long-stop, though Brown was probably the fastest bowler that has ever been known in England. Brown's fieldsmen were placed, nearly all of them, behind the wicket. Once at Lord's a man tried to stop one of Brown's balls with his coat, and the ball passed through his coat (pushing it aside) and killed a dog behind it instantaneously. Brown once

challenged Beldham to a match when the Surrey
batsman was fifty-four years old, and yet Beldham
against this terrific bowling got seventy-two runs,
knocking Brown about so much that the fast bowler
hardly dare bowl within Beldham's reach. This
very tough morsel of humanity did not find cricket
disagree with his health. A friend went to visit
him in April, 1859, in his ninety-third year, and
found him at work in his garden before 8 a.m. It
is said he did not stoop in the least, and required
no stick to walk with. Still more wonderful is the
story of his family. He had thirty-nine children!
twenty-eight by his first wife, all of whom died
young; eleven by his second wife. In 1852 when
he was eighty-six years of age, he walked from
Tilford to Godalming, a distance of seven miles, to
see a match between England and Godalming.
' Silver Billy ' must have deserved his name still
more in his old age. He was the last survivor of the
famous Hambledon Club, a club who brought into
the field an eleven composed of the most famous
players of the last century, and among them Beldham was a shining light. Old Nyren says of him,
' We come to the finest batter of his own, or perhaps
of any age. William Beldham was a close-set,
active man, standing about 5 ft. 8½ in. He had
light-coloured hair, and we called him " Silver Billy."
No one within my recollection could stop a ball
better, or make more brilliant hits all over the
ground. Wherever the ball was bowled, there she
was hit away, and in the most severe, venomous
style. Besides this, he was so remarkably safe a
player ; he was safer than the Bank, for no mortal
ever thought of doubting Beldham's stability. He

received his instruction from a ginger-bread baker, at Farnham, of the name of Harry Hall. . . . He would get in at the balls and hit them away in gallant style ; yet in this single feat, I think I have known him excelled : but when he could cut them at the point of his bat, he was in his glory : and upon my life their speed was as the speed of thought. One of the most beautiful sights that can be imagined, was to see him make himself up to hit a ball. It was the beau ideal of grace, animation and concentrated energy. In this peculiar exhibition of elegance and vigour, the nearest approach to him I think was Lord Frederick Beauclerk. Upon one occasion at Marylebone, I remember these two admirable batters being in together, and though Beldham was then verging towards his climacteric, yet both were excited to a competition, and the display of talent that was exhibited between them that day was the most interesting sight of its kind I ever witnessed. I should not forget, among his other excellences, that Beldham was one of the best judges of a short run I ever knew. As a general fieldsman there were few better : he could take any post in the field ; latterly he chose slip. He was a good change bowler too.'

BISHOP MONTGOMERY.

M.C.C.'s Eulogy of Mr. William Ward (1830)

AND of all who frequent the ground named after
　　Lord,
On the list first and foremost should stand Mr.
　　Ward :

No man will deny, I am sure, when I say
That he's without rival first bat of the day ;
And although he has grown a little too stout,
Even Mathews is bothered at bowling him out.
He's our life-blood and soul in this noblest of games,
And yet on our praises he's many more claims :
No pride, although rich, condescending and free,
A well-informed man, and a City M.P.

Ward and Jenner

I WAS not old enough at that time to take much notice of the style of play of Mr. Ward, the hero of the cricket period, but I once played in a match with him and also with Herbert Jenner, who was an excellent wicket-keeper, though he stood five or six feet behind the wicket and walked forward to meet the ball ! There were no such things as pads or finger-guards in those days :

> ' They didn't mind a few stingers,
> And they didn't wear India-rubber fingers.'

When leg-pads were first introduced they were worn *under* the trousers, as though the hardy cricketer was ashamed of his cowardice in wearing them.

On Mondays, in the more important matches, we saw plenty of the southern players, such as Lillywhite, Pilch and Mynn, but not much of those from the north, beyond the Nottingham men—no doubt on account of the difficulties and expense of locomotion at that time.

SIR SPENCER PONSONBY-FANE, G.C.B.

M.C.C.'s Epitaph on Lillywhite   ∿

LILLYWHITE.

BORN JUNE, 1792 ; DIED AUGUST 21ST, 1854.

A NAME TO BE REMEMBERED LONG AS

THE NATIONAL GAME OF ENGLAND,

BY THE PRACTICE AND TUITION OF WHICH

FOR YEARS HE EARNED AN HONEST LIVELIHOOD.

RARELY HAS MAN RECEIVED

MORE APPLAUSE IN HIS VOCATION.

FEW HAVE ADMINISTERED TO MORE HAPPY HOURS.

FROM AN HUMBLE STATION HE ACHIEVED

A WORLD-WIDE REPUTATION,

TEACHING, BOTH BY PRECEPT AND EXAMPLE,

A SPORT

IN WHICH THE BLESSINGS OF YOUTHFUL STRENGTH

AND SPIRITS MAY BE MOST INNOCENTLY ENJOYED,

TO THE EXERCISE OF THE MIND,

THE DISCIPLINE OF THE TEMPER, AND THE

GENERAL IMPROVEMENT OF THE MAN.

THIS MONUMENT

TESTIFIES THE RESPECT OF

THE NOBLEMEN AND GENTLEMEN OF THE

MARYLEBONE CRICKET CLUB,

AND OF

MANY PRIVATE FRIENDS,

TO ONE WHO DID HIS DUTY

IN THAT STATE OF LIFE TO WHICH IT HAD

PLEASED GOD TO CALL HIM.

Alfred Mynn   ∿   ∿   ∿   ∿   ∿

MR. MYNN was without doubt the most popular
cricketer of his day. When I played with him

towards the end of his career he was always the centre of attraction on every cricket field, and the spectators would crowd about him when he walked round the ground, like flies round a honey-pot. His immense popularity threw even the superior abilities of Pilch and Parr into the shade. He was beloved by all sorts and conditions of men, and he in return seemed to think kindly of every one. He had an affectionate regard for his old fellow-players who had fought shoulder to shoulder with him through his brilliant career, and there are many players who were just becoming known to him in his latter days who could bear witness to the kindness and encouragement he showed to them. As a bowler he was very fast, with a most stately delivery, bowling level with his shoulder. As a batsman he was a fine powerful hitter. He played a driving game, setting himself for this and not cutting much. Against fast bowling he was magnificent, and against slow of an inferior quality he was a great punisher. Against the best slow bowling of the day he did not show to so much advantage. He had not that variety of play which enables a batsman to deal with this sort of bowling to the best advantage. His pluck and gameness were something wonderful, and were shown in every department of the game.

He had an iron constitution which nothing seemed to upset. He liked good living, and seemed especially to enjoy his supper. I have often seen him eat a hearty supper of cold pork and retire to bed almost directly afterwards !

A curious custom of his was taking a tankard of light bitter beer to bed with him during the night.

' My boy,' he once said to me when he saw me taking a cup of tea, ' beef and beer are the things to play cricket on ! '

WILLIAM CAFFYN.

Queer-tempered William Clarke ᔕ   ᔕ

Captain and Secretary of the famous All England Eleven

CLARKE played until he was quite an old man ; and as he had only one eye (the sight of the other having been destroyed at fives), George Parr used to say that in his latter days he played not by *sight* but by *sound*. The old man was very queer-tempered, and was consequently a considerable trial to the patience of many of the younger members of his elevens.

George Parr says there was once a young amateur playing with Clarke for the first time whom he mortally offended. This gentleman, before the game began, asked the veteran where he should field. ' Can you catch ? ' asked Clarke. The amateur having replied that he could, was ordered into the long field, where he shortly had a high catch hit to him from Clarke's slow bowling, which he failed to hold. The old man looked ' unutterable things ' at him, but said never a word. On Clarke's side taking the field in the second innings, this gentleman again asked where he should go. ' Oh ! ' said old Clarke, ' walk about where you like ; there'll be plenty of balls flying about presently, and I dare say you will manage to hold *some* of 'em.'

Clarke always put a stop to all bragging on the part of young players with whom he came in contact. One of his sayings, which speaks volumes, I often quote at the present time : " Fighting in the ring is quite another thing.' This is what Clarke always said to those who often tried to induce him to play young local players in some of his own great matches. This was to remind them that, though these young fellows might be giants amongst their own people, they would find there was a totally different kind of cricket played amongst the chief players of the county in their matches.

Clarke once played off a good joke on some cabmen in London. The All England Eleven were on their way to a match in the south, and while in town they each purchased a new white tall hat. Some cabmen on a stand, seeing eleven men so equipped, began to make jeering remarks about their headgear. Nothing was said in reply ; but after getting some fifty yards away, old Clarke put up his hand. Immediately several of the cabs came tearing up in order to get to him first, but when they reached him the old cricketer assured the drivers he had no intention whatever of taking a cab. When the Jehus began to abuse him in no very choice language, he declared that if, when in London, a man could not hold up his hand in the public street without having a lot of blackguards driving after him and insulting him, the sooner he got back into the country the better he should be pleased.

Once, too, a railway porter tried to get him to leave a non-smoking compartment in which he was enjoying a cigar, and which at first Clarke refused to quit. The porter, placing one hand on the window ledge, waved the other to call the attention of the stationmaster ; and while so engaged, Clarke clapped the lighted end of his cigar on the back of his hand. The porter sent up a howl, but Clarke coolly told him he was merely extinguishing his weed as he had been bidden, and if any harm had come of it, it must be entirely owing to the owner of the hand and not to the owner of the cigar.

The veteran would always insist on going in to bat in one particular place—two wickets down, I think it was—but in a match in which George Parr, instead of himself, was captain, he was put down several places lower on the list. However, when his usual turn came, he stepped out padded and gloved, and the batsman who was next to go in, arriving at the wicket at the same time, was obliged to return to the pavilion. But as years went on the old gentleman dropped down to the last place of all ; and being run out once by the batsman at the other end (old Tom Box) when it came to the second innings he put on his pads to go in *first,* swearing he would never again go in within ten of the fool who had run him out in the previous innings.

RICHARD DAFT.

George Alfred Lohmann

WHEN Surrey ladled out defeat,
    Who did it ?
When Notts and Yorks and Kent were beat,
    Who did it ?
Lohmann did—George Lohmann—

Something like a yeoman,
Neither fast nor slow man,
George !

NORMAN GALE.

W. G. on E. M. Grace ∽ ∽ ∽

ONCE when we were on a tour with the West
Gloucestershire team in Wales, E. M. and I made
a practice of keeping wicket to each other's bowling.
Although I say it myself, we proved pretty good
behind the wickets. But our hands wouldn't
stand the hard treatment, and we gave up the
experiment. As a general rule, I think it's stupid
for a safe batsman or a good bowler to put on the
wicket-keeping gloves, as sooner or later he is
certain to get his hands damaged.

When E. M. was in his prime he was made the
subject of a curious bet. He was playing at Manchester in an All England Eleven against Eighteen of
Manchester. While he was at the wicket—I think
he had made about twenty runs—somebody made
a bet of 20 to 1 that he would not score 100. E. M.
was hitting tremendously hard at the time, and the
man who gave the odds had a very narrow shave of
losing the bet, because when the innings closed
E. M. had made 97 not out. If the last man had
survived another over it was more than probable
the bet would have been lost.

H. D. G. Leveson-Gower on 'W. G.'

WHEN I first had the honour of making his acquaintance, I was introduced to him as 'Shrimp,' a
nickname that has stuck to me closer than my

baptismal name.   That same evening he called me
' Snipe.'   No one else ever has on any occasion.

Coming from such a source, his advice on captaincy
was always invaluable.   I remember his telling
me, just before I left for South Africa in charge of
the England team, never to mind criticism.   He
said : ' No captain was ever worth his salt unless
he was criticized.   When you take on a captaincy,
you take on the criticism it entails as well.'   No
truer remarks were ever made, not only about
cricket, but about other responsibilities in life.

Possibly others may have suggested that as a
captain W. G. adhered to what prevailed in his
young days.   I recollect that he entirely disapproved of the modern idea of giving a mere
change bowler the first turn with the new ball.
' No, no, start your innings with your best bowler
Give him the best chance.   It's the best way to
bowl out the best bats on the other side.'

When I was one of the selection committee for
choosing the England side in test matches against
Australia, W. G. advised me that two left-handed
batsmen ought to be selected.   ' There are so many
good bowlers who cannot bowl well to left-handed
batsmen.   And as any one batsman may fail, why
not have a second left-handed one to bother the
other side ? '

F. R. Spofforth on ' W. G.'

On the occasion of W. G. Grace's first visit to
Australia, I only played in one match against him,
and when I met him in England six years later, he

said : ' I only remember this Demon Bowler as a long, thin fellow, standing in the deep-field and throwing in so terribly hard.'   In those days I practised long shying, and could generally bung in the ball a hundred and twenty-eight yards.

I had a lark with the Old Man at the nets. In those days, though I stood six feet three inches, I only weighed ten stone six. But I could bowl faster than any man in the world. W. G. was at the nets at Melbourne, and I lolled up two or three balls in a funny slow way. Two or three of those round asked, ' What's the matter with you, Spoff ? ' I replied, ' I am going to have a rise out of that W. G.'   Suddenly I sent him down one of my very fastest. He lifted his bat half up in his characteristic way, but down went his off stump, and he called out in his quick fashion when not liking anything : ' Where did that come from ? Who bowled that ? '   But I slipped away, having done my job.

A Canadian Estimate of ' W. G.' (1872)

ONE of the Montreal papers, in referring to my innings, said : ' Mr. Grace is a large-framed, loose-jointed man, and you would say that his gait is a trifle awkward and shambling, but when he goes into the field you see that he is quick-sighted, sure-handed, and light-footed as the rest. He always goes in first, and to see him tap the ball gently to the off for one, draw it to the on for two, pound it to the limits for four, drive it beyond the most distant long leg for six, looks as easy as rolling off

F

a log.' I have had my style and appearance variously described at different times by newspaper reporters, but that reference is, perhaps, the most curious I have ever had made to myself.

W. G. Grace's Jubilee ⌀ ⌀ ⌀

Ah, he has seen where the grass is green
    A host of warriors strive
Since the days of old when, a stripling bold,
    He first stepped out to drive.
When of those who play with him here to-day
    But a few had learnt to creep,
Though some, maybe, on their nurse's knee
    Were lulled with a song to sleep.

His comrades then are grey-haired men,
    Whose fading eyes grow dim
As they call to mind what is left behind
    When they are watching him.
Yet his arm, they vow, is as lusty now,
    His eye is just as keen,
His reach as long, his nerve as strong,
    As when he was but nineteen.

Since he treats each ball as he treated all
    In the days that are no more,
For he cracks the slow of any ' pro '
    To the boundary rails for four ;
Shooters he stops, cuts wide long hops,
    They come to him all the same,
While he lets very few of the fast ones thro'
    When he plays his forcing game.

So every friend at his innings' end—
    May it be a distant day—
Will remember still the Champion's skill,
    How he got that Yorker away !
Nor shall we forget, with a keen regret,
    When his glorious course is run,
To be proud that he was born to be
    Athletic England's son.

The Cricket Record of 'W. G.' ᴄ ᴄ

For the whole of his first-class career

BATTING.

Matches	Innings	Times not out	Highest score	Runs	Average.
878	1,493	105	344	54,896	39.55

BOWLING.

Balls	Runs	Wickets	Average
126,017	51,488	2,864	17.97

Parnell as Cricketer ᴄ ᴄ ᴄ

BEFORE the late Mr. Parnell entered politics, he
was pretty well known in the province of Leinster
in the commendable character of a cricketer. He
was captain of the Wicklow eleven, and in those
days a very ardent cricketer. He was considered
ill-tempered and a little hard in his conduct of that
pastime. For example, when the next bat was not
up to time, Mr. Parnell, as captain of the fielders,
used to claim a wicket. Of course he was within
his right in doing so ; but his doing it was anything
but relished in a country where the game is never
played on the assumption that this rule will be

enforced. In order to win a victory he did not hesitate to take advantage of the strict letter of the law. On one occasion a match was arranged between the Wicklow team and an eleven of the Phœnix Club to be played on the ground of the latter in the Phœnix Park. Mr. Parnell's men, with great trouble and inconvenience, many of them having to take long drives early in the morning, assembled on the ground. A dispute occurred between Mr. Parnell and the captain of the Phœnix team. The Wicklow men wished their own captain to give in and let the match proceed. Mr. Parnell was stubborn, and rather than give up his point marched his growling eleven back. That must have been a pleasant party so returning without their expected day's amusement ; but the captain did not care. In later years Mr. Parnell was to use the Irish party as he used the Wicklow eleven.

A Great Master : Arthur Shrewsbury

THOSE who really understand cricket could appreciate Arthur Shrewsbury, who was a master at all times, but especially so on a sticky wicket. His greatest innings in a Test Match was at Lord's in 1886, when he scored 164, with the ground helping such great bowlers as Garrett, Giffen, Spofforth, and Palmer. He was batting six hours and a half, but his mastery over all the bowling was complete. . . . There never was a harder man to bowl out, and it is said that Tom Wass first attracted attention by bowling Shrewsbury in the nets at Trent Bridge, no one else at that time having bowled him in practice for years.

Shrewsbury was the most modest and unassuming of men, but he played the game with intense earnestness and seriousness.

P. F. WARNER.

Lord Harris ♋ ♋ ♋ ♋

KENT has had many good friends, but the most potent force in the county for many years has been the influence of Lord Harris. In the days when he was one of England's representative batsmen, Lord Harris was a fine, free, forcing player, and also a fine fielder. He has captained an English team in Australia, and was also England's captain in the first Test Match that took place in this country in September, 1880. This match was played at the Oval, and is famous for Dr. W. G. Grace's 152 in England's first innings, and for the late W. L. Murdoch's 153 not out in the second innings of the Australians—even in those far-off days, both players demonstrated that they were not dismayed when they happened to meet with disasters in the earlier portions of the game, but played spiritedly on to the end.

Lord Harris has deservedly earned the deepest regard of all professional cricketers, who recognize how much he has done in their interests. The active part he has taken in the councils of the game since he retired from the field of play has made him a valuable national asset. He greatly increased the prestige of the game in India by playing when he was Governor of the Bombay Presidency, and at first was severely criticised in the native Press for doing so ; but he remained in

India long enough to convince the native upper classes that there was nothing *infra dig.*, even in the Governor of Bombay taking part in a cricket match.

A. A. LILLEY.

Albert Trott ✧ ✧ ✧ ✧ ✧

YOU think of Trott as a bowler, and how would you describe him—you can hardly do it. Trott's fast one, particularly that fast yorker, was a holy terror. It might be followed by a slow off break or a leg break. He was unique in his variety, and he never minded how much he was hit.

More than one youthful cricketer, too, has had to thank Trott for the full toss to leg to complete his first century in first-class cricket. The next ball might spread-eagle the stumps, but it was Trott's kindly spirit that prompted the easy one. . . .

The 'Albatrott' as Rip, who loved to sketch Trott, always called him, was bitterly disappointed because the Australian authorities did not choose him for their side to visit England in 1896. ' Very well,' he said, ' I will go on my own account,' and qualifying for Middlesex, he first played for the county in 1898. . . . His best year was in 1899.

I remember one hot afternoon in July when Middlesex were batting having a chat and a cooler with Trott, and he told me he was going to break all cricket records that season by scoring 1,000 runs and taking 200 wickets. It did not look possible, but he did it for the first time in the history of the game. In all, he made 1,175 runs and took 239 wickets, and the next year he repeated the feat by scoring 1,337 runs and taking 211 wickets. . . .

Few men could tell a good story better than Albert. In a match he was always the life and soul of the professionals' room, and many a well-known cricketer will recall some quaint practical joke played on him by the humorous Australian. . . .

Trott at slip was wonderful. I can see him now, legs wide apart, and perhaps the biggest pair of hands I ever saw, eager for the edged ball. If it came straight to him it was a catch certain, but he made many wonderful catches handling the ball on either side, when many fielders would have turned and looked towards third man and said, ' Yours.'

As a batsman Trott was impatient : he loved to use the long handle and for years had an ambition to break the clock face on the old racquet court and to hit a ball over the pavilion. I do not remember him accomplishing the former feat, but he did carry the pavilion, and to this day holds the record. I forget the match, but I shall never forget the shout that went up from the crowd as the ball sailed over the building. . . .

Trott's biggest score was his 164 for Middlesex against Yorkshire at Lord's in 1899. His greatest bowling feat was accomplished in 1907 in his benefit match, which was against Somerset—how like the man ! he took four wickets with consecutive balls, and later on, in the same innings, did the hat trick. Trott also took all ten wickets against Somerset in 1900 at Taunton.

Trott at one time wrote a weekly article for a periodical of which I was sporting editor, and his racy stories made it one of the best columns of the kind ever turned out by a professional cricketer. . . .

P. J. Moss.

Richardson ○ ○ ○ ○ ○

WHO that saw it will ever forget that wonderful effort of his to win the Test Match at Manchester in 1896. Hour after hour he kept pounding away, and if in the end England just lost the match, defeat in such a struggle was glorious. With a wonderfully serene temperament and the heart of a lion, taking him day in and day out, Richardson deserves to rank as the greatest fast bowler the world has yet seen. . . .

Richardson, indeed, was a fine figure of a man, with his giant build and strength, dark hair, and swarthy countenance.

P. F. WARNER.

'*The Croucher's*' *Début* ○ ○

OF the various lean years which Gloucestershire has at one time and another experienced, 1894 stands out as the leanest in her history. The season was a shockingly wet one, and consequently scoring was abnormally low throughout. But, difficult as the wickets undoubtedly were, the conditions could not be held to be wholly responsible for the repeated collapses of the batting. It was 'W. G.'s' least successful year, though he did head the batting list of the county, with an average of eighteen. In this, my first match, everything was favourable for the batsman, and yet, though Lancashire's first-innings' total was round about three hundred, that was sufficient to inflict defeat upon us by an innings and nearly a hundred runs. Lancashire batted practically the whole day, and gave me my first experience of what a long day in the field feels like. After bowling about thirty overs for over seventy runs, with the single success of an ' l.b.w.' to reward me, my future as a county cricketer did not appear to me, as I wended my way to the pavilion that evening, as over-promising. Evidently ' W. G.' held another opinion, for, as we mounted the steps together, he said : ' Well bowled, young 'un ! ' That was quite sufficient for me, and I went to bed quite happy that night. Naturally, I looked for the next morning's papers with rather more than ordinary interest. Turning to the account of the match, amongst other descriptive matter, I read : ' If Mr. Jessop's batting is no better than his bowling and fielding, he is scarcely likely to become an acquisition to the western shire.'

I had some uncomfortable moments before receiving my first ball in county cricket. Mold was at his fastest that morning, and, in the last over before lunch, two wickets had fallen, Mr. H. H. Francis being run out, and Dr. E. M. Grace failing to connect with a yorker the very next ball. I do not mind confessing that it was the least enjoyable luncheon within my cricket experience, and, I may also add, that the walk to the wicket to face the Lancashire Terror was not altogether a period of unalloyed joy. However, all's well that ends well, and of the insignificant total of ninety odd runs my share was rather more than a quarter. As I also contributed a fair share to the second innings' total, I was booked by the G.O.M. of cricket for the next three matches, and although my inclusion made but small addition to the batting strength of Gloucestershire in those matches, yet, by an occasional catch and an odd wicket or two, I succeeded in keeping my place in the team for the remainder of the month of August. Thanks to the gallant stonewalling tactics of that fine natural left-handed bowler, Roberts—a pillar of strength to Gloucester cricket for many years—the last match of the season, against Somerset at Taunton, gave me my first half-century. With the exception of one innings— and one innings alone—that is the effort which brings to me at this moment the happiest memories.

G. L. JESSOP.

The ' Guv'nor,' Bobby Abel

IT is related of him that once at Lord's in a Gentlemen v. Players match he flinched a bit at Kortright, who with his long springy run up to the wicket could be almost terrifying on a fiery pitch, and being chaffed about it, replied that he had several children and that there were plenty of other bowlers besides Kortright to make runs off !

' Plum ' Warner

EACH famous cricket ground has its own particular idols. The Oval is always associated with Hobbs and Hayward ; Brighton with Fry and Ranji ; Taunton with Palairet and Sammy Woods ; and the chief figure among our sun-splashed memories of Lord's is that of P. F. Warner in his faded Harlequin cap, nervously fidgeting at point, or bearing on his shoulders throughout the heat of a July afternoon the varying fortunes of his side. If ever there was a fine sportsman, he is Captain Warner. He is one of the most graceful of English batsmen ; he captained Middlesex for many years ; he has led the Gentlemen into the field both at Lord's and the Oval ; he has probably scored more centuries at Lord's than any man that has ever lived, more even than W. G. and in 1903 not only did he win for Middlesex the proud position of Champion County, but also captained the M.C.C. team to Australia, and brought back the ' ashes ' with him. And when first-class cricket began in 1919, there was nothing that gave deeper pleasure to lovers of cricket than to see P. F. Warner in the first weeks of the season make one of his most brilliant centuries against the Australians at Lord's. It was a reassuring link with the great traditions of the past—a proof, as it were, that in spite of international turmoil the true spirit of sport was indestructible. Besides playing cricket, Captain Warner has written on the subject more extensively, probably, than any other regular first-class cricketer. His book, *Cricket Reminiscences*, published by Mr. Grant Richards, is a book that will be found on the shelves of all those who care for cricket.

It contains practically all the best of Captain Warner's memories of the cricket-field from the day when, as a small boy in a top-hot and Eton jacket, he was handed over the turnstile at the Oval, and nearly wept when Walter Read was clean bowled by an unknown left-hander. It is full of battles fought out and arms long laid upon the shelf. There is an account of the great test match in 1902, when England was beaten by three runs ; and another of the equally great match when Jessop, Hirst and Rhodes turned an almost certain defeat into a one-wicket victory. In ' Wisden ' one score may read very much like another, but to the genuine cricket enthusiast no two games are alike, and to Captain Warner the cricket field is ever full of fresh adventures.

ALEC WAUGH.

' LORD'S '

Off to Lord's ! ∽   ∽   ∽   ∽

ONE day last summer we were hurrying westward
in the afternoon, when four or five busy gentlemen
rushed past us, making a kind of race for the identical cab to which we were leisurely proceeding,
and, as it happened, for the very same fare. ' Where
to, gentlemen ? ' said the driver to the two insides.
' To Lord's, like fury,' was the curt reply, and off
went the hansom, with a flip under the flank to
start with.

We are now at Lord's. The match is The All
England Eleven v. The United All England Eleven
—very like the ' four-and-ninepenny hat shop '
versus the 'true original four-and-ninepenny hat
shop,' which, after months of recriminating abuse
to attract partisans for each party, proved both
to belong to the same smart Barnum of a man !

How crowded is the field ! You can hardly find
standing room. The ring is three or four deep all
round the ground. Four or five thousand men are
there, each man's visual rays converging, as intently
as at Epsom or at Ascot, to one single point ; and
there they stand, and have been standing, many of
them three or four hours without moving, every
man with mind as abstracted as in sleep, from all
business cares, and with a stream of thought wholly

79

new, and a health-restoring vital current passing through the brain.

A pack of hounds is a blessing to a county. The music of the pack sends a joyous thrill through hundreds who never ride to hounds. Off goes the doctor, down the lane, and overtakes the parson on his cob. The blacksmith has dropped his hammer to climb the nearest hill ; and (as we once knew) the squire's wife leaves the delinquent Abigail half discharged to catch a sight of the dogs, and it is half an hour before she comes, breathless, back to her kitchen to settle with the saucy delighter in perquisites all about the legitimate warning of ' this day month.' But a hunt is nothing to a cricket match, as regards the thousands entertained and ' ripping up the sleeve of care.' At Birmingham, Manchester, or Sheffield, a hundred and twenty pounds have been taken at the gate in sixpences, threepences and pennies, and representing nine or ten thousand eager spectators of the strife.

Sheep at Lord's in Early Days

It is a curious fact that, whenever there is a test match at Lord's, many prominent business men in the city become strangely unwell after luncheon.

There is a glamour about Lord's, the prince of cricket grounds ; but even there Bolshevism has been known to manifest itself. Encroaching on the field of play is generally associated with football matches ; but in 1896, when England was playing Australia, the crowd became so enormous that it invaded the match-ground and, finally, so encroached upon the field of play, that cricket became almost a farce.

THE GREATEST AUSTRALIAN

The first Australian team visited us in 1878, and made cricket history by dismissing the M.C.C. side at Lord's for thirty-three and nineteen respectively, finishing off the match in four and a half hours. Boyle captured nine wickets for seventeen and Spofforth ten for twenty.

Spofforth was the greatest of all Australians. He is the ' W. G.' of the world's bowlers. His pace was terrific ; yet Blackham stood close up to the wicket and took the ball with ease and accuracy, when every miss meant a boundary.

THE FINEST INNINGS

The Australians' smallest score in this country was eighteen, made against the M.C.C. in 1896 ; Pougher, playing for the M.C.C., took five wickets for no runs.

One of the most magnificent innings against the Australians was Shrewsbury's 164 at Lord's in 1886. Lord Harris describes it as ' the finest innings I ever saw. It was an extremely difficult wicket,' he continues, ' and Spofforth was bowling from the Pavilion end, and putting on as much off-break as he pleased.'

SHEEP AS MOWING-MACHINES

Lord's did not always wear the Tyrian purple. In its early days the official mower, for instance, was a flock of sheep, which was penned up on match days. On Saturdays, four or five hundred sheep were driven on to the ground on their way to Smithfield Market. ' It was marvellous,' writes Sir Spencer Ponsonby-Fane in *Lord's and the M.C.C.*, ' to see how they cleared the herbage. From the pitch itself, half a dozen boys picked out the rough stalks from the grass. In those days the pavilion held about forty or fifty people.'

On the ground was a public-house, with a few green benches, on which thirsty spectators sat and smoked long pipes]as they enjoyed their drinks and the cricket. Round the ground there were more of these small benches, without backs, and a pot-boy walked round with a supply of beer and porter for such of the public as desired to refresh themselves.

A Shilling a Pitch

But for a square patch of grass opposite the pavilion, which was kept constantly rolled, the ground was an affair of ridges and furrows, not improved by the number of old pitches which abounded. In those days anyone could have a pitch for a shilling, a sum which included the use of stumps, bat and ball.

The ordinary cricket dress of the day was a flannel jacket of short cut and a tall-hat. The creases were cut with a knife which, if more distinct than the whitening now used, was scarcely calculated to improve the ground.

Dedication to the M.C.C.

My Lords and Gentlemen,—Duly impressed with frequent Repetition of your Goodness, I have, with the most profound Deference, presumed to offer this small, but I flatter myself, useful Tract, of the most important article of performing that useful and Noble Game of Cricket. Conscious of your Kindness, I thus fearless approach you, being fully convinced that, however trifling the Subject, when due exertions have been attempted, you will not cast, hurtfully, to the performer, the futile attempt; under such impressions, my Lords and Gentlemen, I have devoted a portion of time in penning those Articles which may guide the inexperienced to the full Attainment of the Knowledge which may be conducive to their Satisfaction, while it advances their Health, which, that you may ever enjoy, is the earnest wish of, my Lords and Gentlemen,

Your devoted and obedient Servant,

T. BOXALL.[1]

The First Round-Arm Bowler ◌ ◌

IN 1822 Mr. John Willes, said to be the inventor of round-arm bowling, came to Lord's with the far-famed Kent Eleven. He had frequently assisted in first-class matches, and often bowled amidst great uproar and confusion, though he would persist until the ring closed round him and stumps were lawlessly pulled up. Thinking, perhaps, that his delivery would receive due consideration if introduced at Lord's, he opened the attack for the hop county with the round-arm delivery. His anticipations were very soon shattered, and after being no-balled by the umpires, Noah Mann, jun., and Henry Bentley, he left the ground in high dudgeon, vowing he would never play again.

A. D. TAYLOR.

Pilch and Lillywhite ◌ ◌ ◌

ONCE at Lord's, whilst waiting for Pilch to come in to bat, some one exclaimed aloud, ' Hullo, " Lilly," here comes your master,'—whereupon the old man

[1] This was written in 1800.

G

turned round with celerity and exclaimed, ' I wish
I had as many pounds as I have got out Pilch ! '
Sometimes, as a joke, he would be put in the long-
field in order to see him *bowl* back the ball, for his
delivery in fielding was identical with that of his
bowling.

' This may have resulted,' wrote Lord Charles
Russell, ' from his extreme jealousy of the cunning of
his right hand, as he would often refuse a hard
chance of c. and b. with the remark, " Ha ! where
would you be without my " bowwling " ? '   On one
occasion at Lord's, when the captain had shouted
to him, " Now then, wake up, and try to catch
somebody from your bowling," Thoms recalled
" Lilly," who was nettled, replying, " Look here, sir,
when I've *bowled* the ball *I've done with hur*, and I
leaves hur to my field ! " '

The Fire at Lord's   ᴄ   ᴄ   ᴄ

ABOUT one o'clock on Friday morning a fire broke
out in the pavilion in Lord's Cricket Ground, and,
from its being built of wood, it burnt with such
fury that the whole was reduced to a heap of ruins
before it was possible for the fire-engines to render
any assistance. The pavilion was, at a great expense,
lately enlarged and decorated for the accommoda-
tion of the various Clubs who frequent this ground ;
and, with the exception of the foundation, nothing
now remains.   There was in the pavilion a large
and valuable stock of wine, the property of the
subscribers, which, along with all their cricketing
apparatus, now no longer exists.   Mr. Neale, the
landlord of the tavern adjoining the ground, cannot

account for the accident, for there never was any
fire in the pavilion during the season, beyond a
lighted candle to enable gentlemen to smoke their
cigars. Such, however, was the strength and power
of the fire at its height, that some of the trees in
the adjoining gardens have been damaged.

' *Byron's Match* ' ✆ ✆ ✆ ✆

(Eton *v.* Harrow, August 2, 1805.)

LORD BYRON, in one of his letters, has an interesting
reference to the match. ' We have played Eton,'
he wrote, ' and were most confoundedly beat ;
however, it was some comfort to me that I got
eleven notches in the first innings and seven in the
second, which was more than any of our side, except
Brockman and Ipswich, could contrive to hit.
After the match we dined together and were extremely friendly ; not a single discordant word was
uttered by either party. To be sure, we were most
of us rather drunk, and went together to the Hay-
market, where we kicked up a row. . . . How I got
home after the play, God knows ! '

It will be seen that Byron states his scores at seven
and eleven, but, according to the printed and generally
accepted account, he made only seven and two.
Charles Lloyd, the Harrow captain in 1808, made the
remark to Dean Merivale (who has repeated it in his
Recollections, that ' Byron played in the Eleven, and
very badly too. He should never have been in the
Eleven had my counsel been taken.' His Lordship
was lame, and had Stratford Canning—afterwards
Lord Stratford de Redcliffe—to run for him.
' Though Byron was lame,' said one of his Harrow

schoolfellows, ' he was a great lover of sports, and preferred hockey to Horace, relinquished even Helicon for duck-puddle, and gave up the best poet that ever wrote hard Latin for a game of cricket on the common.' The victorious Etonians after the match addressed the following epigram to their opponents :

'Adventurous *boys* of Harrow *School*,
  Of cricket you've no knowledge ;
You play not cricket, but the fool
  With *men* of Eton College.'

Byron, it is said, on behalf of Harrow, sent the following reply :

'Ye Eton wags, to play the fool
  Is not the boast of Harrow School ;
What wonder then at our defeat ?
  Folly like yours could ne'er be beat.'

The poet's name, with the date 1805 attached, can be seen in the Fourth Form room at Harrow, above those of Sir Robert Peel (afterwards Prime Minister), Cardinal Manning, and Lord Palmerston.

A Lord's Wicket of 1868

HAD I been a wicket-keeper or a batsman at Lord's during the late match[1], I should have liked (*plus* my gloves and pads) to have worn a single-stick mask, a Life Guardsman's cuirass, and a tin stomach-warmer. The wicket reminded me of a middle-aged gentleman's head of hair, when the middle-aged gentleman, to conceal the baldness of his crown,

[1] Gentlemen *v.* Players, W. G. Grace scoring 134 (not out).

applies a pair of wet brushes to some favourite long
locks and brushes them across the top of his head.
So with the wicket. The place where the ball
pitched was covered with rough grass wetted and
rolled down. It never had been, and never could
be, good turf. I send a specimen or two for your
inspection.

I have no hesitation in saying that in nine
cricket-grounds out of ten within twenty miles of
London, whether village green or county club
grounds, a local club could find a better wicket, in
spite of drought and in spite of their poverty, than
a Marylebone Club supplied to the Players of England.

F. GALE.

Centuries at Lord's

WHY do I sing of Cricket ? Ask no more.
White is the Hope of Cricket, white its Lore—
The fragrance of all things is of the core.
Why do I sing of Cricket ?—Cast the Score.

* * * * *

They say old Homer once set up the Sticks
In Paradise, and Dante made a Six ;
Then SHAKSPERE, that great Player—the red ball
Smote, and a Planet flamed across the Styx.

Some for the Limelight pine upon the Boards,
Some for Green Benches and a spate of words,
And some for Slabs of Gold. Give not a damn—
'Tis SUMMER—we'll have Centuries at Lord's.
A shady seat at Lord's, an even score,
Nine wickets down, and only one ball more,

With Jessop crouching, and with Trumble on—
And what were all Golconda to a FOUR !

GEORGE FRANCIS WILSON.

Lord's in 1902 [1] ✍ ✍ ✍ ✍

THE season's cricket at Lord's has produced some curious incidents, for which the Manchester, Sheffield, and Lincolnshire Railway must be held mainly responsible. We do not refer to the haze of smoke which has prevented half the matches being finished. That is now an accepted condition of the game. Nor does the loss of three of the ground men by fatal accidents on the railway exceed the average mortality of recent years. It is well known that no Insurance Company will insure the life of anyone playing at Lord's ; but it is idle to expect a fieldsman, anxious to save runs and keen in his pursuit of the ball, to go round by the bridge instead of crossing the line. Fogs and fatalities, however, are matters of course : and since a well-known amateur was killed while fielding at long-off by a ginger-beer bottle thrown from the window of a passing train, experienced players always elect to field at the pavilion end. The committee, in view of the frequency of accidents, will during the winter months consider the advisability of treating the railway-line as a boundary, though the ground will in that case be so much curtailed that a boundary hit will only count two runs. It is thought, however, that the row of memorial stones erected to the memory of

[1] This article, printed in the *St. James's Gazette* in 1892. gave an imaginary picture of Lord's ' twenty years after.'

players killed by various mishaps will soon form a complete and efficient boundary.

But we allude rather to the incidents affecting the games themselves. The feat of the veteran J. T. Hearne in taking all ten Surrey wickets for 3 runs, by bowling his fastest when trains were passing behind his arm, has been much discussed. Unfortunately he was committed for trial for assault, a ball bowled by him from the other end having passed the wicket-keeper and broken the window of a carriage and the head of a passenger inside. The magistrate in sending Hearne for trial remarked that the prisoner might take bails, but he (his worship) could not. Hearne was eventually acquitted, but was thus prevented from playing in the second half of the season. It will be remembered, too, that the Yorkshire match against the M.C.C. was delayed for a day owing to the attempt of the Yorkshiremen, whose train was late, to save time by leaving it while in motion as it was crossing the ground. They were arrested and taken to the police station. The Hon. A. Lyttelton, Q.C., who was hastily instructed for the defence, admitted that the accused had committed an error of judgment in jeopardizing valuable lives, but urged that the motive was consideration for the public who were waiting on the ground. The prisoners were released on payment of a fine, but were also, of course, unable to play till next day.

But perhaps the most curious occurrence was the victory won by the Australians against England in one hit. It will long be remembered that Australia, winning the toss, sent in Giffen and Lyons, and the latter, driving Lohmann's first ball hard, it fell on to the 11.35 express for Sheffield. The batsmen, of course, ran ; and the fieldsmen saw that it was hopeless to attempt to recapture the ball, which fell through the window of the guard's brake. The Englishmen cried 'Lost ball' ; the umpire, however, ruled that a ball is not lost when you know where it is. After consultation it was decided to telegraph to the station master to return the ball, and subsequently Mr. Stoddart was sent by the 1.10 train to recapture what our sporting contemporaries still call the 'pilule.' The 1.10 is a slow train, and on arriving in the evening at Sheffield Stoddart found to his mortification that the station master had sent the ball back by parcel-post. The parcel did not reach Lord's till 1.30 the next day. Persons on the ground will not easily forget that the Englishmen sat waiting in front of the pavilion while the batsmen continued to run.

When the weapon of attack was again secured, Australia had scored 1849, and the innings was declared closed. The score read thus :

AUSTRALIA—*First Innings*

Lyons, not out	.	.	.	. 1849
Giffen, not out	.	.	.	. 0

Total (innings declared closed) . 1849

Lohmann's bowling analysis read :

O.	M.	R.	W.
0·1	0	1849	0

The Englishmen naturally failed to equal this gigantic total, but it was felt that the luck had been to some extent against them.

' Lord's ' ⌒ ⌒ ⌒ ⌒ ⌒

(From *The Hill*, by Horace Annesley Vachell, by permission of the author and of Mr. John Murray.)

THE Eton Eleven walked towards the wicket, loudly cheered, Cæsar came up in his pads, carrying his bat and gloves. He shook hands with the Caterpillar, and said with a groan that he had to take the first ball.

' Keep cool,' said the Caterpillar. ' The bowling's weak ; I have it from Cosmo Kinloch. They're in a precious funk.'

' So am I,' said the Duffer.

' But you're a bowler,' said Desmond. ' If I get out first ball, I shall cut my throat.'

But Cæsar looked alert, cool, and neither under- nor over-confident.

' You'll cut the ball, not your throat,' said the Duffer. Cutting was Cæsar's strong point.

The Caterpillar nodded and spoke oracularly :

' My governor says he never shoots at a snipe without muttering to himself, " Snipe on toast." It steadies his nerves. When you see the ball leave the bowler's hand, you say to yourself, " Eton on toast." '

' Your own, Caterpillar ? '

' My own,' said the Caterpillar, modestly. ' I don't often make a joke, but that's mine. Pass it on.'

The other Harrovian about to go in beckoned to Desmond.

' Cæsar won't be bowled first ball,' said the Caterpillar. ' He's the sort that rises to an emergency. Can't we find a seat ? '

They sat down and watched the Eton captain placing his field. Desmond and his companion were walking slowly towards the wickets amid Harrow cheers. The cheering was lukewarm as yet. It would have fire enough in it presently. The Caterpillar pointed out some of the swells.

'That's old Lyburn. Hasn't missed a match since '64. Was brought here once with a broken leg! Carried in a litter, by Jove! That fellow with the long white beard is Lord Fawley. He made 78 *not out* in the days of Charlemagne.'

'It was in '53,' said the Duffer, who never joked on really serious subjects; 'and he made 68 not 78. He's pulling his beard. I believe he's as nervous as I am.'

Presently the innumerable voices about them were hushed; all eyes turned in one direction. Desmond was about to take the first ball. It was delivered moderately fast, with a slight break. Desmond played forward.

'Well played, sir! Well pla-a-ayed!'

The shout rumbled round the huge circle. The beginning and the end of a great match are always thrilling. The second and third balls were played like the first. John could hear Mr. Desmond saying to Warde: 'He has Hugo's style and way of standing—eh?' And Warde replied, 'Yes; but he's a finer batsman. Ah-h-h!'

The first real cheer burst like a bomb. Desmond had cut the sixth ball to the boundary.

Over! The new bowler was a tall, thin boy with flaxen hair.

'That's Cosmo Kinloch, Fluff's brother,' said John. 'I wonder they can't do better than that.

Even I knocked him all over the shop at White Ladies last summer.'

' He's come on, they tell me,' said the Caterpillar. ' Good Lord, he nearly had him first ball.'

Fluff's brother bowled slows of a good length, with an awkward break from the off to the leg.

' Teasers,' said the Caterpillar, critically. ' Hullo! No, my young friend, that may do well enough in Shropshire, not here.'

A ball breaking sharply from the off had struck the batsman's pad ; he had stepped in front of his wicket to cut it.   Country umpires are often beguiled by bowlers into giving wrong decisions in such cases, not so your London expert.   Cosmo Kinloch appealed—in vain.

' He'll send a short one down now,' said John. ' You see.'

And, sure enough, a long hop came to the off, curling inwards after it pitched.   The Eton captain had nearly all his men on the off side.   The Harrovian pulled the ball right round to the boundary.

' Well hit ! '

' Well pulled ! '

' Two 4's ; that's a good beginning,' said the Duffer.

A couple of singles followed, and then the first ' 10 ' went up amid cheers.

' Here's my governor,' said the Duffer.   ' He was three years in the Eleven and Captain his last term.'

' You've told us that a thousand times,' said the Caterpillar.

The Rev. Septimus Duff greeted the boys warmly. His eyes sparkled out of a cheery, bearded face. Look at him well.   An Harrovian of the Harrovians this. His grandfathers on the maternal and paternal side had been friends at Harrow in Byron's time. The Rev. Septimus wore rather a shabby coat and a terrible hat, but the consummate Caterpillar, who respected pedigrees, regarded him with pride and veneration. He came up from his obscure West Country vicarage to town just once a year— to see the match. If you asked him, he would tell you quite simply that he would sooner see the match and his old friends than go to Palestine; and the Rev. Septimus has yearned to visit Palestine ever since he left Cambridge; and it is not likely that this great wish will ever be gratified. He is the father of three sons, but the Duffer is the first to get into the Eleven. . . .

Another round of cheers proclaimed that '20' had gone up. Both boys were batting steadily; no more boundary hits; a snick here, a snack there —and then—merciful Heavens !—Cæsar has cut a curling ball 'bang' into short-slip's hands.

Short-slip—wretched youth—muffs it ! Derisive remarks from the Rev. Septimus.

'Well caught ! Well held ! Tha-a-nks !'

The Caterpillar would pronounce this sort of chaff bad form in a contemporary. He removes his hat.

'Phew-w-w !' says he. 'It's very warm.'

Cæsar times the next ball beautifully. It glides past point and under the ropes.

Early as it is, the ground seems to be packed with people. Glorious weather has allured everybody. Stand after stand is filled up. The colour becomes kaleidoscopic. The Rev. Septimus, during the brief interval of an over, allows his eyes to stray

round the huge circle.   Upon the ground are the
youth, the beauty, the rank and fashion of the
kingdom, and, best of all, his old friends.   The
Rev. Septimus has a weakness, being, of course,
human to the finger-tips.   He calls himself a
laudator temporis acti.   In his day the match was
less of a function.   The boys sat round upon the
grass ; behind them were the carriages and coaches
—you could drive onto the ground then !—and
here and there, only here and there, a tent or a small
stand—*Consule Planco*—the dear man loves a
Latin tag—the match was an immense picnic for
Harrovians and Etonians.   And, my word, you
ought to have heard the chaff when an unlucky
fielder put the ball on the floor.   Or when a batsman
interposed a pad where a bat ought to have been.
Or if a player was bowled first ball.   Or if he
swaggered as he walked, the cydosure of all eyes,
from the pavilion to the pitch.   Upon this subject
the Rev. Septimus will preach a longer (and a more
interesting) sermon than any you will hear from
the pulpit in Blackford-Orcas Church.

Loud cheers put an end to the parson's reminiscences. Desmond's companion has been clean bowled
for a useful fifteen runs.   He walks towards the
pavilion slowly.   Then, as he hears the Harrow
cheers, he blushes like a nymph of sixteen, and begins
to run.   Last year he made ' duck ' in his first
innings, and five in the second.   No cheers then.
This is his first taste of the honey mortals call
success.   He had faced the great world, and captured its applause.

' When does Scaife go in ? ' the Rev. Septimus
asks.

' Third wicket.'

More cheers as the second man in strolls down the steps. A careful cove, so the Duffer tells his father—one who will try to break the back of the bowling.

' They're taking off Fluff's brother,' the Caterpillar observes.

A thick-set young man holds the ball. He makes some slight alteration in the field. The wicket-keeper stands back; the slips and point retreat a few yards. The ball that took the first wicket was the last of an over. Desmond has to receive the attack of the new bowler.

The thick-set Etonian, having arranged the off side to his satisfaction, prepares to take a long run. He holds the ball in the left hand, runs sideways at great speed, changes the ball from the left hand to the right at the last moment, and seems to hurl both it and himself at the batsman.

' Greased lightning ! ' says John.

A dry summer has made the pitch rather fiery. The ball, short-pitched, whizzes just over Cæsar's head. A second and a third seem to graze his cap. Murmurs are heard. Is the Eton bowler trying to kill or maim his antagonist ? Is he deliberately endeavouring to establish a paralyzing ' funk ' ?

But the fourth ball is a ' fizzer '—the right length, a bailer, terrifically fast, but just off the wicket. Desmond snicks it between short slip and third man ; it goes to the boundary.

' That's what Cæsar likes,' says the Duffer. ' He can cut behind the wicket till the cows come home.'

' Cut—and come again,' says the Caterpillar. The fifth ball is played forward for a risky single.

The Rev. Septimus forgets that times have changed.
And if they have, what of it? He hasn't. His
deep vibrant voice rolls across the lawn right up
to the batsman:

'Steady there! Steady!'

And now the new-comer has to take the last ball
of the over—his first. Alas and alack! the sixth
ball is dead on to the middle stump. The Harrovian
plays forward. Man alive, you ought to have played
back at that! The ball grazes the top edge of the
bat's blade and flies straight into the welcoming
hands of the wicket-keeper.

Two wickets for 33.

Breathless suspense, broken by tumultuous
cheers as Scaife strides on to the ground. His bat
is under his arm; he is drawing on his gloves.
Thousands of men and as many women are staring
at his splendid face and figure.

'What a mover!' murmurs the Rev. Septimus.

Scaife strides on. Upon his face is the expression
John knows so well and fears so much—the con-
sciousness of power, the stern determination to be
first, to shatter previous records. John can predict
—and does so with absolute certainty—what will
happen. For six overs the Demon will treat every
ball—good, bad, and indifferent—with the most
distinguished consideration. And then, when his
'eye' is in, he will give the Etonians such leather-
hunting as they never had before.

And so it comes to pass. Wickets fall, Harrovians come and go, but Scaife remains. As he
warms to his work, he seems to expand. It is a
Colossus batting, not a Harrow boy. The balls
come down the pitch; the Demon's shoulders and

chest widen ; the great knotted arms go up—crash !
First singles ; then twos ; then threes ; and then
boundary after boundary. To John—and to how
many others ?—Scaife has been transformed into a
tremendous human machine, inexorably cutting
and slicing, pulling and drawing—the embodied
symbol of force, ruthlessly applied, indefatigable,
omnipotent.

The Eton captain, hopeful against odds, puts on
a cunning and cool dealer in ' lobs.' Fluff is in,
playing steadily, holding up his wicket, letting the
giant make the runs. The Etonian delivers his
first ball. Scaife leaves the crease. Fluff sees the
ball slowly spinning—harmless enough till it pitches,
and then deadly as a writhing serpent. Scaife will
not let it pitch. The ball curves slightly from the
leg to the off. Scaife is facing the pavilion——

A stupendous roar bursts from the crowd. The
ball, hit with terrific force, sails away over the green
sward, over the ropes, over the heads of the spectators, and slap on to the top of the pavilion.

A sixer ! And one of the finest swipes ever seen
at Lord's. Shade of Mynn, come forth from the
tomb to applaud that mighty stroke !

But the dealer in lobs knows that the man who
leaves his citadel, leaves it, sooner or later, not to
return. In the hope that Scaife, intoxicated with
triumph, will run out again, he pitches the next
lob too much up—a half-volley. Scaife smiles.

John's prediction has been fulfilled. A record
has been established. Never before in an Eton
and Harrow match have two ' sixers ' been hit in
succession. The crowds have lost their self-
possession. Men, women, and children are becoming

delirious. The Rev. Septimus throws his ancient topper into the air ; the Caterpillar splits a brand-new pair of delicate grey gloves. Upon the tops of the coaches, countesses, duchesses—ay, princesses—are cheering like Fourth Form boys.

The Harrow first innings closed with 289 runs . . . The Elevens have finished lunch and are mixing with the crowd. Scaife is talking with a famous Old Carthusian, one of the finest living exponents of cricket, sometime an ' International ' at football, and a D.S.O. The great man is very cordial, for he sees in Scaife an All-England player. Scaife listens, smiling. Obviously he is impatient to begin again. As soon as possible he collects his men, and leads them into the field. One can hear the policemen saying in loud, firm voices, ' Pass along, please ; pass along ! ' As if by magic the crowds on the lawn melt away. In a few minutes the Etonians come out of the pavilion. The sun shines upon their pale blue caps and sashes, and upon faces slightly pale also, but not yet blue. For Eton has a strong batting team, and Scaife and Desmond have proved that it is a batsman's wicket. . . .

Presently the first wicket falls ; then the second soon after. And the score is only 20. The Rev. Septimus is beaming ; the Bishop seated beside him looks as if he were about to pronounce a benediction ; Charles Desmond is scintillating with wit and good humour. Visions of a single innings' victory engross the minds of these three. They are in the front row of the pavilion, and they mean to see every ball of the game.

But soon it becomes evident that a determined

H

stand is being made. Runs come slowly, but they come ; the score creeps up—30, 40, 50. Fluff goes on to bowl. On his day Fluff is tricky, but this apparently is not his day. The runs come more quickly. The Rev. Septimus removes his hat, wipes his forehead, and replaces his hat. It is on the back of his head, but he is unaware of that. The Bishop appears now as if he were reading a new commination—to wit, 'Curséd is he that smiteth his neighbour ; curséd is he that bowleth half volleys ! ' The Minister is frowning ; things may look black in South Africa, but they're looking blacker in St. John's Wood

One hundred runs for two wickets.

The Eton cheers are becoming exasperating. A few seats away Warde is twiddling his thumbs and biting his lips. Old Lord Fawley has slipped into the pavilion for a brandy and soda.

At last !

Scaife takes off Fluff and puts on a fast bowler, changing his own place in the field to short slip. The ball, a first ball and very fast, puzzles the batsman, accustomed to slows. He mistimes it ; it grazes the edge of his bat, and whizzes off far to the right of Scaife, but the Demon has it. Somehow or other—ask of the spirits of the air, not of the writer—somehow his wonderful right hand has met and held the ball.

' Well caught, sir, well caught ! '

' That boy ought to be knighted on the spot, says Charles Desmond. Then the three generously applaud the retiring batsman. He has played a brilliant innings of 68, and restored the confidence of all Etonians.

The Eton captain descends the steps ;   a veteran this, not a dashing player, but sure, patient, and full of grit. He asks the umpire to give him middle-and-leg ; then he notes the positions of the field.

' Whew-w-w-w ! '

' D——n it ! ' ejaculates Charles Desmond. Bishop and parson regard him with gratitude. There are times when an honest oath becomes expedient. The Eton captain has cut the first ball into Fluff's hands, and Fluff has dropped it ! Alastair Kinloch, from the top of the Trent coach, screams out,' Jolly well muffed ! ' The great Minister silently thanks Heaven that point is the Duke's son and not his.

And of course the Eton captain never gives another chance till he is dismissed with a century to his credit. Meantime five more wickets have fallen. Seven down for 191 ! Eton leaves the field with a score of 226 against Harrow's 289. Harrow goes in without delay, and one wicket is taken for 13 runs before the stumps are drawn. Charles Desmond looks at the sky.

' Looks like rain to-night,' he says anxiously.

And so ends Friday's play.

The morrow dawned grey, obscured by mist rising from ground soaked by two hours' heavy rain. You may be sure that all our friends were early at Lord's, and that the pitch was examined by thousands of anxious eyes. The Eton fast bowler was seen to smile. Upon a similar wicket had he not done the famous hat-trick only three weeks before ? The rain, however, was over, and soon the sun would drive away the filmy mists. No man alive could foretell what condition the pitch would be in after a few hours of blazing sunshine. The Rev. Septimus told Charles Desmond that he considered the situation critical, and although he had read the morning paper, he was not alluding even indirectly to South African affairs. Charles Desmond said that, other things being equal, the Hill would triumph ; but he admitted that other things were very far from equal. It looked as if Harrow would have to bet upon a treacherous wicket and Eton on a sound one.

At half-past ten punctually the men were in the field. Scaife issued last instructions. ' Block the bowling ; don't try to score till you see what tricks the ground will play. A minute saved now may mean a quarter of an hour to us later.' Cæsar nodded cheerfully. The fact that the luck had changed stimulated every fibre of his being. And he said that he felt in his bones that this was going to be a famous match like that of '85—something never to be forgotten. . . .

Three wickets for 41 !

A quarter of an hour later Fluff was bowled by a yorker. He had made eleven, and kept up his wicket during a crisis. Harrow cheered him loudly.

And then came the terrible moment of the morning. Scaife went in when Fluff's wicket fell. The ground had improved, but it was still treacherous. The fast bowler sent down a straight one. It got under Scaife's bat and spread-eagled his stumps.

The wicket-keeper knows what the Harrow captain said, but it does not bear repeating. Every eye was on his scowling, furious face as he returned to the pavilion ; and the Rev. Septimus scowled also, because he had always maintained that any Harrovian could accept defeat like a gentleman. Upon the other side of the ground the Caterpillar was saying to his father, ' I always said he was hairy at the heel.'

It was admitted afterwards that the Duffer's performance was the one really bright spot in Harrow's second innings. Being a bowler, he went in last but one. It happened that Fluff's brother was in possession of the ball. It will never be known why the Duffer chose to treat Cosmo Kinloch's balls with utter scorn and contempt. The Duffer was tall, strong, and a tremendous slogger. Nobody expected him to make a run, but he made twenty in one over—all boundary hits. When he left the wickets he had added 38 to the score, and wouldn't have changed places with an emperor. The Rev. Septimus followed him into the room where the players change.

' My dear boy,' he said, ' I've never been able to give you a gold watch, but you must take mine ; here it is, and—God bless you ! '

But the Duffer swore stoutly that he preferred his own Waterbury.

Eton went in to make 211 in four hours, upon a wicket almost as sound as it had been upon the Friday. Scaife put the Duffer on to bowl. The Demon had belief in luck

' It's your day, Duffer,' he said. ' Pitch 'em up.'

The Duffer, to his sire's exuberant satisfaction, pitched 'em up ' so successfully that he took four wickets for 33. Four out of five ! The other bowlers, however, being not so successful, Eton accumulated a hundred runs. The captains had agreed to draw stumps at 7.30. To win, therefore, the Plain must make another hundred in two hours ; and three of their crack batsmen were out.

After tea an amazing change took place in the temper of the spectators. Conviction seized them that the finish was likely to be close and thrilling ; that the one thing worth undivided attention was taking place in the middle of the ground. As the minutes passed, a curious silence fell upon the crowd, broken only by the cheers of the rival schools. The boys, old and young alike, were watching every ball, every stroke. The Eton captain was still in, playing steadily, not brilliantly; the Harrow bowling was getting slack.

In the pavilion the Rev. Septimus, Warde, and Charles Desmond were sitting together. Not far from them was Scaife's father, a big, burly man with a square head and heavy, strongly-marked features. He had never been a cricketer, but this game gripped him. He sat next to a world-famous financier of the great house of Neuchatel, whose sons had been sent to the Hill. Run after run was added to the score. Scaife's father turned to Neuchatel.

' I'd write a cheque for ten thousand pounds,' he said, ' if we could win.'

Lionel Neuchatel nodded. ' Yes,' he muttered, ' I have not felt so excited since Sir Bevir won the Derby.'

In the deep field Desmond was standing, miserable because he had nothing to do. No balls came his way ; for the Eton captain had made up his mind to win this watch with singles and twos. Very carefully he placed his balls between the fielders ; very carefully his partner followed his chief's example. No stealing of runs, no scoring off straight balls, no gallery play—till victory was assured. . . .

Once more the Etonian smote, and smote hard ; but this ball was not quite the same as the first, although it appeared identical. The ball soared up and up. Would it fall over the ropes ? Thousands of eyes watched its flight. Desmond started to run. Golconda to a sixpence on the ball ! It is falling, falling, falling.

' He'll never get there in time,' says Charles Desmond.

' Yes he will,' Warde answers savagely.

' He has ! ' screamed the Rev. Septimus. ' He—has ! '

Pandemonium broke loose. Grey-headed men threw their hats into the air ; peers danced ; lovely women shrieked ; every Harrovian on the ground howled. For Cæsar held the ball fast in his lean brown hands !

The Eton captain walks slowly towards the pavilion. He has to pass Cæsar on his way, and passing him he pauses.

' That was a glorious catch,' he says, with the smile of a gallant gentleman.

And as Harrow, as cordially as Eton, cheers the retiring chieftain, the Caterpillar whispers to Mrs. Verney :

' Did you see that ? Did you see him stop to congratulate Cæsar ? '

' Yes,' says Mrs. Verney.

' I hope Scaife saw it two,' the Caterpillar replies coolly. ' That Eton captain is cut out of whole cloth ; no shoddy there, by Jove ! '

And Desmond ?   How does Desmond feel ?   It is futile to ask him, because he could not tell you if he tried.   But we can answer the question.   If the country he wishes to serve crowns him with all the honours bestowed upon a favoured son, never, *never* will Cæsar Desmond know again a moment of such exquisite, unadulterated joy as this.

Six wickets down, and 39 to get in less than half an hour !

Every ball now, every stroke, is a matter for cheers derisive or otherwise.   The Rev. Septimus need not prate of golden days gone by.   Boys at heart never change.   And the atmosphere is so charged with electricity that a spark sets the firmament ablaze.

Seven wickets for 192.

Eight wickets for 197.

Signs of demoralization show themselves on both sides.   The bowling has become deplorably feeble, the batting even more so.   Four more singles are recorded.   Only ten remain to be made, with two wickets to fall.

And twelve minutes to play !

Scaife puts on the Duffer again.   The lips of the Rev. Sep are seen to move audibly.   Is he praying or cursing, because three singles are scored off his son's first three balls ?

' Well bowled—well bowled ! '

A ball of fair length, easy enough to play under all ordinary circumstances, but a ' teaser ' when tremendous issues are at stake, has defeated one of the Etonians.   The last man runs towards the pitch through a perfect hurricane of howls.   Warde rises.

' I can't stand it,' he says, and his voice shakes

oddly. ' You fellows will find me behind the Pavvy after the match.'

' I'd go with you,' says the Rev. Septimus in a choked tone, ' but if I tried to walk I should tumble down.'

Charles Desmond says nothing. But, pray note the expression so faithfully recorded in *Punch*— the compressed lips, stern frowning brows, protruded jaw. The famous debater sees all fights to a finish, and fights himself till he drops.

Seven runs to make, one wicket to fall, and five minutes to play !

Evidently the last man has received strenuous instructions from his chief. The bowling has degenerated into that of anæmic girls—and two whacks to the boundary mean Victory. The new-comer is the square, thick-set fast bowler, the worst bat in the Eleven, but a fellow of determination, a slogger and a run-getter against village teams.

He obeys instructions to the letter. The Duffer's fifth ball goes to the boundary.

Three runs to make and two and a half minutes to play !

The Duffer sends down the last ball. The Rev. Septimus covers his eyes. O wretched Duffer ! O thou whose knees are as wax, and whose arms are as chop-sticks in the hands of a Griffin ! O egregious Duff ! O degenerate son of a noble sire, dost thou dare at such a moment as this to attack thine enemy with a—long hop ?

The square, thick-set bowler shows his teeth as the ball pitches short. Then he smites and runs. Runs, because he has smitten so hard that no hand, surely, can stop the whirling sphere. Runs—aye—and so does the Demon at cover-point.   This is the Demon's amazing conjuring trick—what else can you call it ? And he has practised it so often that he reckons failure to be almost impossible.   To those watching he seems to spring like a tiger at the ball.   By Heaven ! he has stopped it—he has snapped it up ! But if he dispatches it to the wicket-keeper, it will arrive too late.   The other Etonian is already within a couple of yards of the crease.   Scaife does not hesitate.   He aims at the bowler's wicket towards which the burly one is running as fast as legs a thought too short can carry him.

He aims and shies—instantaneously.   He shatters the wicket.

'How's that ? '

The appeal comes from every part of the ground.

And then, clearly and unmistakably, the umpire's fiat is spoken :

'Out !'

The Rev. Sep rises and rushes off, upsetting chairs, treading on toes, bent upon being the first to tell Warde that Harrow won.

'*Io !   Io !   Io !*'

BATTING

The Joy of Batting ∽ ∽ ∽

BATTING may be called the most enjoyable feature of the great and glorious game of cricket. A man even in full training invariably feels the effect of fatigue after bowling sixty or seventy overs, and fieldsmen go through the same experience during a long outing. But it may with truth be said that the keen pleasure which is realized by every cricketer worthy of the name, while he is actually at the wickets, prevents him from feeling fatigue as an inconvenience until the innings is over. We do not believe, though with bated breath let it be said, that the fine rider on a fine horse in a good position and over a grass country with a burning scent can feel so supremely content with the world and its glorious surroundings while galloping and jumping close to hounds, as does a batsman who feels himself master of the bowling on a good wicket in a first-class match, with a fine day and a large crowd keenly anxious for his well-doing. He is conscious that his side is gaining a glorious victory by his efforts, and life can give him no prouder moments. To the young cricketer let us therefore say, in conclusion, that, as the pleasure is so intense and the excitement so keen, he should strive to attain proficiency by care, practice, and the advice of great masters

Above all, he must cultivate the moral qualities that of necessity must have a place in such a great, glorious, and unsurpassable game as cricket.

The Hon. R. H. Lyttelton.

Step in and Hit ◡ ◡ ◡ ◡

I HAVE trained many a youngster (and there is no difference in teaching cricket to the village baker's or carpenter's son, or a duke's) with the aid of a good professional who can bowl well, ' on the lines that Fuller Pilch taught, and Felix, whom I knew well, wrote. And what a trainer should try to do is to teach a boy to *hit* loose balls as well as defence, but not by blind swiping ; and if he has got into a good free defence he ought not to be checked if he sees a ball a little overpitched, and steps in and hits her right away. Who is to say that there are not moments in a boy's life when quickness of hand and eye, backed by courage and a broad pair of shoulders, do not authorize a little risk ?

F. Gale.

Tom Hayward, The Half-Cock Stroke and a Straight Bat ◡ ◡ ◡

THE great Tom Hayward was an exponent of this particular stroke, and writing of him reminds us what a beautiful player he was with his feet ; in his back play particularly he used to pull that right foot of his back on the stumps like a streak of lightning, and down came the blade on the ball with the full broad face of it presented to the bowler. There is nothing so demoralizing to a bowler and so disheartening as to bowl all day at a man who every time offers him the broad face of his bat; it is probable that the poor bowler will turn round and say the well-known words, 'Well! it's like bowling at a brick wall.' Yes; but it is not the *batsman* that is the brick wall. It is his *bat*! The bat to the tired bowler looks like the broad expanse of a wall; so the straight bat has not only the *practical effect* of defending the wicket to greater advantage, but also the moral effect of disheartening the bowler.

D. J. KNIGHT.

A Beautiful Leg-Bye

ACCORDING to Mr. Bettesworth, V. E. Walker used to tell a good story about Dean, a well-known professional player of the past. Dean had been suddenly sent from Lord's to umpire in a match at the Oval, and on his arrival was asked, ' How's the match at Lord's going on ? ' ' Oh, capitally,' he replied, ' Lord C—— and Mr. —— 'as been in for 'arf an hour; they gets no runs, but just as I left the ground his lordship kicked a beautiful leg-bye.'

An American Poet on Jessop

(*A Match with the Gentlemen of Philadelphia*)

AT one end stocky Jessop frowned,
  The human catapult
Who wrecks the roofs of distant towns
  When set in his assault.

* * * * *

Now Jessop's eye was eagle bright,
His courage beat full high
And he set out to demonstrate
That ' Demon ' King was ' pie.'

RALPH D. PAINE.

An Injured Irishman   ↶   ↶   ↶

THAT gentleman hailed from Cork who, on another occasion, anticipated the umpire's verdict. He had received what the bowler imagined to be a straight yorker on the end of his boot.

' How that ? ' with one accord from bowler and wicket-keeper.

' Moighty painful, if it's me you're asking. You've killt the taw of me entirely ! ' and dropping his bat he hopped about holding the injured member.

Our umpire on the occasion did not come from Scotland, and, being a soft-hearted man, took a lenient view of the transaction. The supposed cripple, a most cheery and amusing cricketer, not only compiled a respectable score, but ran short runs like a hare. He was caught in the country at last, and was well on his way to the pavilion when he found that he had forgotten to reclaim the ' sweater ' which after the first ten minutes he had entrusted to the umpire's keeping. As I went to meet him with the sweater I could not resist an inquiry as to the condition of the injured ' taw.' ' Sure I had forgotten it entairely,' and with that he put on the most comical limp all the way back to the pavilion.

W. E. COLLINS.

Taking it Easy   ∽   ∽   ∽   ∽

A FAT squire, an enthusiast in the game of cricket, although so afflicted with the gout as scarcely to be able to stand, nevertheless could not do without his daily bat practice.   So he sat on a stool beside the wicket ready for the bowler, who was cautioned not to bowl at his legs.   A tramp, not knowing him, and thinking him too idle for the work, said, ' Why, master, you are as fat and lazy as the old gardener's dog who leaned against the wall to bark.'

AN OLD CRICKETER.

Great Moments : Batting ∽   ∽   ∽

LIFE has many great moments to offer us—moments which are of supreme joy, and which are never forgotten by those who experience them.   The recollection of these moments recurs from time to time, and becomes more precious as the years roll by.   They bring a thrill to the heart of him who has just conjured up before him a vision of that moment of triumph, now so long ago.   These memories are ever with us, and no misfortune or mischance can blot their precious image from our minds.   To the great painter, the thought of his first work accepted by the Academy will be his most abiding memory ;   to the great archæologist, the remembrance of that last spadeful of earth thrown aside and the first few stones of a long-buried city at last exposed to view ;   to the big-game hunter, the thought of his first tiger slain ; and to the cricketer, the vivid recollection of his first century for his county, or perhaps the memory

of a single isolated stroke, when the ball went off
the bat to the boundary at such tremendous speed
and with that indescribable feeling that only batsmen can know and appreciate—the sign of a perfectly timed stroke, with brain, eye, wrist, and bat
working in complete unison.

D. J. KNIGHT

The First Cricket Triolet

I STEPPED in to drive,
    And the umpire said, ' Out, Sir ! '
Being last of the hive
I stepped in to drive,
For we wanted but five,
    And had made them, no doubt, Sir,
But I stepped in to drive,
    And the umpire said, ' Out, Sir ! '

COULSON KERNAHAN

A Parody of Tennyson [1]

BLOCK, block, block,
    At the foot of thy wicket, O Scotton !
And I would that my tongue could utter
    My boredom. You *won't* put the pot on !
Oh, nice for the bowler, my boy,
    That each ball like a barn door you play !
Oh, nice for yourself, I suppose,
    That you stick at the wickets all day !

And the clock's slow hands go on,
    And you still keep up your sticks ;

[1] W. Scotton batted sixty minutes *v.* Australia without
scoring.

But oh for the lift of a smiting hand,
  And the sound of a swipe for six !
Block, block, block,
  At the foot of thy wickets, ah, do !
But one hour of Grace or Walter Read
  Were worth a week of you !

A Sixer [1]

AN instant, poised in air,
A rosy light delayed ;
Dropt, and a willow blade
Flashed like a golden share,
Flashed—and a throbbing star
Waned to a spark, afar !

GEORGE FRANCIS WILSON

Pegging Away !

THE truth must be insisted on ; many a cricket
match has been won in the bedroom. And even
with the ball a good deal may be done. I could
name two eminent batsmen who used, as boys, to
wait after the day's play was over, and the careless
crowd had departed, and in the pavilion give ten
minutes or a quarter of an hour to practising a
particular style of defence, the one bowled fast
sneaks along the floor to the other, at about ten
paces distance. This, too, yielded fruit in its time.
Like all other great achievements, the getting a
score against good bowling is the result of drudgery,
patiently, faithfully borne. But the drudgery of
cricket is itself a pleasure, and let no young cricketer

[1] From *Cricket Poems*, by permission of the Author.

I

suppose that he can dispense with it, though some few gifted performers have done great things with apparently little effort.

HON. EDWARD LYTTELTON.

The Young Batsman   ∽   ∽   ∽

ANY fool can play forward, but it is only the good player who can score off forceful back strokes. The young player should master the defensive back stroke for the purpose of keeping his wicket intact before attempting the scoring back stroke. Learn discretion in regard to balls you hit and those you should leave alone. When you first go in, and the ball is anything approaching a length, leave it alone if it will pass the wicket without hitting it. You then get a sight of it, and can also gauge the pace of the wicket. I always used to advise my bowlers to make a batsman play at the ball when he first came in, which is only possible if the ball is more or less straight. When batting against a bowler who is making the new ball swerve away it is most important to leave as many balls as possible, with any length about them, severely alone. In all cutting of the ball, get the bat up quick, shoulder high, when you are in a position to leave the bat on your shoulder if the ball passes too high, or, if the right height, you are still correctly balanced to come down on the ball for runs. One must always be truly balanced in every kind of stroke. Correct footwork is half the secret of successful batting. Wipe out everything that is incorrect. If you are to have consistent success you must always remain correct in your forward and back

play, and also in your hitting.   Towards the end
of a practice boys like to indulge in a bit of hitting,
and no harm is done provided they hit correctly
and not across the line of the ball.   Never draw
away from the wicket, and remember that when
the ball is breaking on to the body a batsman will
score off it by bringing his right foot back in front
of the wicket, for he has then made it a leg ball ;
but should he draw away the ball will chase him
and hit him.   This is the most difficult ball for
youngsters to overcome.   Every boy can gain a
certain measure of success as a batsman if he will
follow advice from his coach, who knows the game,
and then strengthen his own natural strokes, using
his head throughout.

A. C. Maclaren

Eight Bowlers and Ten Bats   ∽   ∽

I do not know the nationality of the young gentleman who, with all a schoolboy's bright candour,
expressed to a great cricketer, the captain of a
side that went down to Sandhurst, his gratification
that the cadets were at last to meet foemen worthy
of their steel.

' You know,' he exclaimed, ' we have got a most
wonderful side here this year.   Quite the best we
have ever had.   We really have got eight bowlers
and ten bats.'

' That sounds like a very strong side indeed,'
was the courteous answer.

Yet I am afraid that there was a trace of equally
courteous irony in the leave-taking.   It was only
a one day's match, played before the ' declaration '

rule had come into operation, and the boys had not won the toss.

'Well, good-bye,' said the visiting captain, 'and thank you very much for a most enjoyable day. We have seen the eight bowlers, and I only wish we could come again and see the ten bats.'

W. E. COLLINS.

BOWLING

A Cricket Bowler ∽ ∽ ∽ ∽

Two minutes' rest till the next man goes in !
The tired arms lie with every sinew slack
On the mown grass. Unbent the supple back,
And elbows apt to make the leather spin
Up the slow bat and round the unwary shin—
In knavish hands a most unkindly knack ;
But no guile shelters under this boy's black
Crisp hair, frank eyes, and honest English skin.
Two minutes only. Conscious of a name,
The new man plants his weapon with profound
Long-practised skill that no mere trick may scare.
Not loth, the rested lad resumes the game :
The flung ball takes one madding tortuous bound,
And the mid-stump three somersaults in air.

EDWARD CRACROFT LEFROY.

' Throwing Instead of Bowling ' ∽

THE first we hear of round-arm bowling was by
Tom Walker about 1785, who, quoting from Nyren,
' began the system of throwing instead of bowling,
now so much the fashion. At that time it was
esteemed foul play, and so it was decided by a council
of the Hambledon Club called for the purpose.
The first I recollect seeing revive the custom was

Willes, a Sussex man.' This was about 1805, and in Sutton Valence Churchyard in Kent there is a tombstone to Mr. John Willes, and on it is recorded : ' He was a patron of all manly sports, and the first to introduce round-arm bowling in cricket.'

There is a story that he got the idea from his sister when practising in a barn, and, being short of players, induced his sister to bowl to him. She being obliged from her dress to bowl with her hand out from her side, Willes found her deliveries puzzling, and started to bowl that way himself. William Lillywhite and James Broadbridge began bowling round-arm in a first-class match, Sussex *v.* All England, played at Brighton in 1827. The law was then that the hand must be below the elbow. But Lillywhite and Broadbridge continued to bowl as before, and found so many followers that the M.C.C. passed the motion brought forward by Mr. Knight. The rule as to the hand being below the shoulder was re-affirmed in 1845. It was not till 1864 that bowlers were allowed to raise the arm above the shoulder.

A Bowling Record ∽ ∽ ∽ ∽

JOHN WISDEN, playing for England *v.* XXII of the United States and Canada, at Rochester, U.S.A., in 1859, took six wickets in six balls. But James Walker for Ashcombe Park *v.* Tunstall in 1882, and James Stebbing playing for Frindsbury *v.* Rainham in 1902, both took eight wickets in eight balls.

Human Natur' in the Cricket Ball ∽

' AY, there's a deal o' human natur' in a treble-seam, sir ; it don't like getting knocked about any more than we do.'

E. W. HORNUNG.

Old Tom Emmett ∽   ∽   ∽   ∽

AT one time Tom was engaged with a local club in Yorkshire, and in one match catch after catch was dropped with such systematic persistence that he threw the ball on the ground and said : ' I am not going to ball any more ; there's an epidemic on this ground, but, thank God, it ain't *catching*.'

A Long-Hop to Leg ∽   ∽   ∽

To a casual and impartial observer that which goes by the name of King's Langley Common would suggest itself as an admirable site for a hydropathic establishment, hospital, or sanatorium—nay, even for a croquet-ground or bowling-green, or in short for pretty well anything you like save only a bathing-place or a cricket-ground, Yet there some enthusiast, in despair, possibly, of finding a field on the flat, did at some time in the dark ages lay out a cricket-ground, and, with certain reservations, not a very bad cricket-ground either. True, the wickets are pitched on the top of a high hill so inconveniently near a steep declivity that deep square-leg at one end, if he stands in his proper place, has to take a good deal of what is happening upon the higher level for granted, and counts himself fortunate if he gets an occasional view of cover-point on the sky-line.   But the pitch

is good.   On such a ground, then, King's Langley
were contending against a rival local team under a
hot August sun, and things were not going very well
for the home side—for the terror of the neighbourhood, a really free and stylish batsman, was making
considerable hay with the bowling.   Whether owing
to initial nervousness or impatience, Tom W——
was a bad starter, and only got firmly set once in
a way throughout the course of the whole season.
On this day, no style of bowling seemed to come
amiss to him ; and the King's Langley captain, as
plucky an old cricketer as ever donned flannels—
not particularly clean flannels, by the way—was
fairly at his wits' end.

'You don't bowl by any chance, Mr. H—— ? '
he exclaimed, addressing the wicket-keeper, a
cheery-hearted young gentleman whose name as a
matter of fact began with an E.

It is nothing more or less than throwing tempta-
tion at a man's head to ask him who has been
alternately crouching behind the wicket, or hopping
round it for four mortal hours by the clock on a
boiling hot August day, whether he would like a
change of occupation.

'Bowl ? Of course I bowl,' and the wicket-
keeper's pads and gloves were off in a moment.
Ready enthusiasm is often contagious. It proved
to be so then. The old captain's eye brightened
up ; weary fieldsmen of a sudden waxed more
sprightly ; only one dissentient voice was heard.
Did it come from a disappointed bowler or the
cynical ex-parson, who used to field point ?

'You are quite sure, old chap, that you've got
an action ? '

'Half a dozen,' was the prompt reply ; 'here, chuck me the ball'—and taking advantage of the circumstance that the batsman had temporarily retired to what in that part of the world we used to call the 'drinking-hovel,' the wicket-keeper embarked upon a series of trial balls by way of discovering which particular action among the alleged half-dozen was best adapted to the wicket and the occasion.

'I knew,' he confessed to me afterwards, 'that it was only a case of one over when it really came to business, so I thought I might as well try whether I could make the beastly ball do anything beforehand.'

Presently the captain, who, after watching the bewildering series of trial balls, had begun to doubt whether he really had unearthed a treasure, suggested that perhaps Mr. H—— would like to place his own field. This the new bowler did after a fashion entirely his own, planting a sort of silly short-leg somewhere in front of the umpire, ordering the deputy wicket-keeper to stand well back, and putting everybody else on the off-side.

'Over the wicket, sir, or round ?' inquired the bowler's umpire.

'Whichever you like—over, no, I mean round.'

He took a tremendously long run, and then sent down the slowest and worst long-hop to leg that I ever saw. 'Look out on the leg side,' he shouted. Short-leg and the umpire threw themselves flat on their backs in order to escape utter destruction ; all the men on the off-side sat down, feeling that they had no further interest in the match ; and Tom, after making one or two remarks to the wicket-

keeper while he was waiting for the ball, spat on
his hands and hit it right down to the bottom
of the hill, where the tinker's dog ran away with it.

W. E. COLLINS.

The Hat Trick ◇ ◇ ◇ ◇

ALL Song is of the *Heart*; its breath is not
Of THIS you *have* or THAT you *haven't got*:
Equal to them whose secret souls rejoice
Are Cobbled-alley and smooth Garden-plot.

Cæsar had Joys enow—Respect his bones!—
And Cæsar had his Pride. But think of Jones
Who with sequential balls has late o'erthrown
The Brightest and the Best that Clapham owns.

He left the City's bound by ten-to-Three—
The green fields called to him, and he was free—
He left the City's bound. By Four-fifteen
The Cap of all his dreams he held in fee!

GEORGE FRANCIS WILSON

Brahma [1]   ◇ ◇ ◇ ◇ ◇

(After Emerson).

IF the wild bowler thinks he bowls,
  Or if the batsman thinks he's bowled,
They know not, poor misguided souls,
  They too shall perish unconsoled.
I am the batsman and the bat,
  I am the bowler and the ball,
The umpire, the pavilion cat,
  The roller, pitch, and stumps, and all.

ANDREW LANG.

[1] By permission of Messrs. Longmans, Green & Co.

The Glorious Uncertainty ∽ ∽

PEOPLE who do not play cricket are sometimes apt to grumble at the amount of chance that enters into the game ; as a matter of fact I think no game can take the highest rank unless it has two essential qualifications : it must give scope for unlimited skill and unlimited chance. Take either of these away and you lower your game into the second rank. For this reason, chess, though a great game, cannot be put quite in the first rank. Two games take the lead absolutely of all others—one for indoors, the other for the open air : *whist* and *cricket.* There are no games which so completely combine skill and chance.

I have never seen the uncertainty of cricket better shown than in the Universities Match of 1870. Oxford was in for the second time ; there were three wickets to fall and four runs to get ! Many persons left the ground supposing the match was over : and so it was, but not as they expected ! Mr. Butler, the Oxford batsman, made a hard hit to leg which would have certainly gone for four had it not been half stopped by Mr. Ward's right hand, a left-handed bowler. Three runs to get and three wickets to fall ; over is called : then Mr. Cobden bowls to Mr. Butler. Off the first ball Mr. Butler was caught at middle wicket. The next ball produced no results. Two more balls to the over and two men to defend the wickets and two runs to make it a tie ! Cobden's next ball bowled the last man but one. It was Stewart (I think), the Oxford wicket-keeper, who then marched to the wickets to save his University from disaster ; I wonder if he knew whether he

walked on his head or his heels ; to me it seemed
as if Cobden rushed up to deliver his last ball with
a ferocious energy ; the ball was straight ; Stewart
hit wildly to square leg, and Cambridge won.

BISHOP MONTGOMERY.

To Helen [1] ⌀ ⌀ ⌀ ⌀ ⌀

(After seeing her bowl with her usual success)

HELEN, thy bowling is to me
    Like that wise Alfred Shaw's of yore,
Which gently broke the wickets three :
    From Alfred few could smack a four :
        Most difficult to score !

The music of the moaning sea,
    The rattle of the flying bails,
The grey sad spires, the tawny sails—
    What memories they bring to me,
        Beholding thee !

Upon our old monastic pitch,
    How sportsmanlike I see thee stand !
The leather in thy lily hand,
    O Helen of the yorkers, which
        Are nobly planned !

ANDREW LANG.

C. B. Fry on Rhodes ⌀ ⌀ ⌀

How does the batsman see Wilfred Rhodes ?
Hostile meaning behind a boyish face—ruddy and
frank ; a few such easy steps and a lovely swing
of the left arm, and the ball is doing odd things at

[1] By permission of Messrs. Longmans, Green & Co.

the other end ; it is pitched where you do not like
it, you have played forward when you do not want
to—you have let fly when you know you ought
not ; the ball has nipped away from you so quickly ;
it has come straight when you expected break ;
there is discomfort.

Wilfred Rhodes' Birthday

(June 13, 1877)

ONE of our conquerors.—MEREDITH.

From Yorkshire come, and will come, the giants
of the field.—BERNARD WHELAN.

York thrives to beat.—SHAKSPEARE.

We will hear of Wilfred to-day or to-morrow.—
MEREDITH.

Twist cunningly.—DICKENS.

And Twist has become a nuisance ; . . . when
he comes, we go.—DICKENS.

I have heard men talk of Mr. Peel.—PRAED

And welcome waterspouts.—MEREDITH.

Ducks on the green.—RANDOLPH CALDECOTT.

On Certain Bowlers

I

SHOULD a cricketer whose anecdotes are apt to be
crusted and egotistical embark upon a story commencing, ' Once, when I was bowling——' you may,
perhaps, feel yourself justified in interrupting him
to ask politely, ' Were you captain ? ' He will
probably decide to tell his story to some one
else.

II

As manager of a side you will have failed in your duty if you engage even the honestest man as bowler purely on his own recommendation. You must always bear in mind that bowlers are infinitely less frequent than bowlo-maniacs.

III

Mr. S—— was a frequent captain of elevens in South Devon. The Reverend Mr. A—— was a constant player—an excellent bat, and a sufferer from bowlo-mania of a very malignant type. Mr. S—— would never allow him an opportunity of showing his prowess. But, on a day in August, when Mr. S—— was absent at his shooting-box in the Highlands, the Reverend gentleman had his golden opportunity. He was captain, and, needless to say, bowled. To the surprise of all present— save one—he secured three wickets for seventeen runs. This analysis he immediately telegraphed to Mr. S—— in Scotland. Mr. S——'s shooting-box was seventeen miles distant from the telegraph station. The telegram was sent out by a man on foot. When the messenger arrived the dogs were loose in the courtyard. They were hungry and telegraph messengers are always attractive to canine nature.

They tore the breeks from the trewed Highlander, who had to be consoled with whisky and broadcloth.

To learn of the success of the Rev. Mr. A——'s bowling cost Mr. S—— a bottle of whisky, seventeen shillings porterage, and the price of a pair of trousers.

HORACE G. HUTCHINSON.

The Art of Bowling: Practice and Hard Work ∽ ∽ ∽ ∽ ∽

IT is often said that bowlers are born, not made, and the statement is partly true. Spin and intelligence, which are both essential for a bowler's success, are natural gifts. Bowling does not require the same combination of hand, foot and eye as batting, but it does demand more practice and greater powers of initiative. A good slow or medium-paced bowler must use his head. The only man who can dispense with ' head-work ' is the crack fast bowler. Tom Richardson, with his tremendous speed and natural break back, obtained over a thousand wickets in four years, without any study of tactics, and without a change of pace ! Yet many good judges place Lockwood above Richardson as a fast bowler, on account of the slow ball he so cleverly concealed.

Length, the foundation of all bowling, is not a natural gift. Length can and must be acquired by practice. In the case of professionals, who have to bowl for a living, length becomes automatic, but few amateurs have absolute control of pitch.

The majority of cricketers who play for pleasure prefer batting to bowling, and shirk the hard work which is the only road to accuracy of length. That great batsman and coach, Mr. R. A. H. Mitchell, used to say that everybody ought to try to learn to bowl. ' No one can be sure that he will not turn out a bowler until he has practised in vain for a considerable time.'

Of course there have been and are amateurs, known and unknown to fame, who practise bowling.

Many students of cricket know that Mr. M. Kempson and Sir Frederick Bathurst bowled unchanged through the Gentlemen v. Players match in 1853, but fewer know that Mr. Kempson, who was a fast bowler, practised bowling for two hours a day for six weeks before the match.

Mr. David Buchanan, after bowling fast left hand for eighteen years, changed to slow left hand, and by steady practice in the winter immediately rose to the front rank in his new style. Between 1868–1874 in ten Gentlemen v. Players matches, he took eighty-seven wickets, and in 1878, when forty-eight years old, was invited by Lord Harris to go with his team to Australia. Mr. Arthur Appleby, the great Lancashire bowler, also attributed his success to constant practice.

Mr. E. M. Dawson, up to the age of fourteen, used to bowl for half an hour a day in the holidays, even in the winter, and on one occasion had his bowl after 28 degrees of frost ! At seventeen, when at Harrow, he was fit to bowl for the Gentlemen. Unfortunately he afterwards learned to bat.

Hard work alone enabled Mr. Bosanquet to develop his invention, the ' googly ' or ' off-breaking leg-break,' which was so successfully imitated by Mr. Schwarz and the South Africans, and also by Mr. D. W. Carr. Mr. Carr frankly admits that he practised for two winters and a cricket season before he got a length for both breaks.

E. R. WILSON

THE POETRY OF CRICKET

Proem ∽ ∽ ∽ ∽ ∽ ∽

CRICKET, of games the rose of all that please
Whether in London city or beneath
Far Austral skies, or on some village heath,
No name of promise and past ecstasies,
Of sun-spaced hours and green-grass memories
Falls from our lips with such as easeful breath
When Spring hath laid aside her girlish wreath
And Summer's tresses float upon the breeze !

Nor gold may stain, nor tyrant qualify
Thy Commonweal of Peace : thy votaries,
Whose song is healing and whose regimen
A rhythmic unison 'twixt hand and eye,
For their reward do ask but twilight ease,
For their last law the law of honest men.

GEORGE FRANCIS WILSON.

The Poets of Cricket [1] ∽ ∽ ∽

' My song shall be cricket. and cricket my theme.'
—JOLLY, *The Cricket Enthusiast.*

THE aristocracy of verse, the hierarchy of the
Poets' Corner, have neglected the national game.

[1] From *At the Sign of the Wicket*, by E. B. V. Christian,
by permission of the author.

Yet the theme should have inspired them.   By all
the definitions cricket should be the source of melody.
Is poetry a 'criticism of life'?   Cricket shows
life at its highest and best.   There is a lyric ecstasy
in the bowler when, 'fit' and full of battle, he
runs to the crease.   Does poetry consist of the
'best words in the best place'?   Then 'not out'
is the very soul of poetry.   'The best general
notion I can give of poetry,' said Hazlitt, 'is that
it is the natural impression of any object or event
by its vividness exciting an involuntary movement
of imagination and passion, and producing by sympathy a certain modulation of the voice or sounds
expressing it.'   Who that has heard the deep thun-
derous cheer at the Oval can doubt the 'involuntary
passion' of the spectators, the vividness of the
impression the struggle creates, or fail to note the
varied 'modulations of the voice or sounds' uttered
by the throng, from the rolling cheer that greets a
boundary-hit to the groan of despair as a hero's
wicket falls?   Here, one would say, is a subject to
be hailed by even the monarch of the major bards.

Yet a few casual allusions, some poor stray
gleanings, are all that can be culled from the
plenteous harvest of English verse.   The game is
seen but obliquely, a chance object in the back-
ground.   Hood introduces his cricketers—boys
'as sportive deer'—merely for contrast to the
moody Eugene Aram.   Pope and Cowper have but
frigid references to the game ; Crabbe speaks in a
single line of the swains

'Who struck with matchless force the bounding ball,'

and therefore, doubtless, gave catches.   It is the

way of the untutored agricultural batsman. Lord
Tennyson had but one or two allusions; a Laureate
should have given at least a volume to so patriotic
a theme. His longest reference is hardly accurate :

> ' A herd of boys with clamour bowled,
>   And stumped the wicket . . .'

Bowlers sometimes, though rarely, clamour, but
certainly a herd of boys could not all be bowling
at once. And what is ' stumped the wicket ' ?
It is, surely, the batsman who is stumped. Another
bard suggests a reason for the poets' reticence.
People would not stand it, he thinks,

> ' If devotees of football and of cricket
>   Should clog the press with innings and with maul,
>   And rabid scribes be always on the wicket,
>   Or always on the ball.'

Calverley, addressing the undergraduates of a
younger generation, recalls his mighty youth :

> ' I have stood serene on Fenner's
>   Ground, indifferent to blisters,
> While the Buttress of the period
>   Bowled me his peculiar twisters.'

Yet Calverley classed cricket as merely one among
many sports, with rat-catching, wine parties, and
the driving of dog-carts.
        . . . So large a canvas as these early portraits fill
could hardly be allowed to all the artists. But
one other match, at least, stands recorded for our
instruction, in verse and at length. Middlesex v.
Bucks, in 1864, was described by ' William Wilson,
a professor of music ' :

'My song is of a cricket match, as great as e'er was seen,
  'Twixt Buckingham and Middlesex, two right good teams
    I ween,
On August fourth, and fifth, and sixth, on wickets short
    and green :
The year was Eighteen-sixty-four, the weather was
    serene,
When this famous cricket match was played these
    Counties good between.

Now Buckingham did win the toss, and Leigh did quick
    begin,
With Golby opposite, to try a noble score to win,
But Golby sent a ball direct into Ned Pooley's fin ;
Next Dupuis, bowled by V. E. Walker, left with a
    ghastly grin,
               When this famous, etc.'

The 'ghastly grin,' one may surmise, is one of
those ideas which Dryden says are often suggested
by the need of a rhyme ; and it is singular how
often cricket poets, like Calverley, feel bound to
'mention again it was glorious weather.' Less
'correct' than Love, Mr. Wilson was more realistic.
One famous player is unkindly described :

                  'Thomas Hearne,
A famous cricketer, tho' rather heavy in the stern.'

Nearly a thousand runs were made in the match,
as the poet notes, and Middlesex won, after following on in a minority of 218, so that the poet should
not have lacked for inspiration. The Harrow and
Eton match of 1865 called less loudly for the bard,
and he was mercifully brief in his adaptation of
'Hohenlinden.'

The changes that time brings naturally call for
comment, and the inveterate tendency of mankind
to find degeneration in everything, from the weather

to the Constitution, has not spared the English
game. The introduction of round-arm bowling
was so fruitful a cause of discussion that it is not
surprising to find the poet dissatisfied. In the time
of Budd and Lord Frederick, he says :

> ' The ball was bowled, no slingy round stuff then;
> 'Tis all up now, the game's transmogrified.'

Another laments the time :

> ' When gentlemen who played at cricket
> Were content with a proper height wicket.
> * * * * *
> When their legs wer'n't all padding,
> Nor their arms all wadding,
> And they didn't mind a few stingers,
> And they never wore India-rubber fingers.'

' I'll sing a song,' says another, ' of the good
old underhand.' But most of the cricket bards
come to praise the game, not bury it ; they are
in the best of humours ; a fine patriotism leads
them to contemn the sports of other nations, and
proudly challenge comparison. ' Floreat Cricket,'
says ' Begley ' :

> ' 'Tis a grand institution, deny it who can,
> By the world is acknowledged its fame ;
> Long live each true Briton who'll play like a man
> At cricket—our national game.'

As for golf, football, and the like, pooh !—cricket
is the game :

> ' 'Twill be played in old England for hundreds of years
> When tennis and such like are gone to the wall.'

The game, these poets say, promotes good feeling,
it levels ranks, it gives health, it prevents quarrels.

. . . 'The Song of the Fast Bowler,' in *Wickets in the West*, goes to a familiar tune :

> ' Stand to your stumps, the toss is won,
> I shall bowl you all out ere the day is done :
> Breathes the Kanuk who can withstand
> The ball as it leaves my big left hand ?
> Field, brothers, field, my rapids are near
> To the sticks, and the shooters a way will clear.'

The recent revival of ladies' cricket suggests to 'L. S.' some ' mixed criticisms ' :

> ' Maud at point you cannot beat,
> Nellie's great at saving byes ;
> Olive s cuts are rather neat,
> Phyllis—has the sweetest eyes.'

Another Nelly—Mr. R. B. Brough's 'Neighbour Nelly '—combined all the charms :

> ' You should see her play at cricket
> With her little brother Jim.'

As a rule, it is not to incidents in the game, but to the praise of the game at large, or of clubs or famous players, that the poet tunes his lyre. A song in Mr. Hutchinson's *Creatures of Circumstance* ' to a well-known and noble tune, " Tramp, tramp, tramp, the boys are marching," ' is perhaps less well known than it deserves to be :

> ' What Englishman can dare
> Any pastime to compare
> With the great and grand old manly game we love ?
> What sight so sweet to view
> As a wicket hard and true,
> And the fieldsmen kept for ever on the move ?

Chorus.

Run, run, run, the ball's a-rolling,
    Scarcely to the boundary she'll go ;
And the throwing's getting wild, and the wicket-keeper's
    riled,
    So we'll try to steal another for the throw.'

*   *   *   *   *

Of one cricketer who has gone, the only man who
bulked as large upon his time as Dr. Grace on
ours, we have something like a worthy memorial.
The verses are by S. Maunder (W. J. Prowse), whose
last act ere his own death, we are told in *Cricketers
in Council*, was to write an article on the decease
of Lockyer, Pooley's predecessor at the Oval :

Jackson's pace is very fearful, Willsher's hand is very
    high,
William Caffyn has good judgment and an admirable eye ;
Jemmy Grundy's cool and clever, almost always on the
    spot ;
Tinsley's slows are often telling, though they sometimes
    catch it hot ;
But however good their bowling, pitch or pace, or break
    or spin,
Still the monarch of all bowlers, to my mind, was Alfred
    Mynn.

' Richard Daft is cool and cautious, with his safe and
    graceful play ;
If George Griffiths gets a loose one, he can send it far
    away ;
You may bowl your best at Hayward, and whatever
    style you try
Will be vanquished by the master's steady hand and
    certain eye.
But whatever fame and glory these and other bats may
    win,
Still the monarch of good hitters, to my mind, was
    Alfred Mynn.

*   *   *   *   *

'With his tall and stately presence, with his nobly-
    moulded form,
His broad hand was ever open, his brave heart was ever
    warm ;
All were proud of him, all loved him.   As the changing
    seasons pass,
As our hero lies a-sleeping underneath the Kentish grass,
Proudly, sadly, we will name him—to forget him were a
    sin,
Lightly lie the turf upon thee, kind and manly Alfred
    Mynn ! '

An Old Cricket Hymn

LET those who want to plaie the game
    To Fuller Pilch attende,
What he tolde me I'll tell the same
    To all who ears will lende.

Five yards behinde ye stumps first stande,
    And let ye umpire bee
Where he doth judge ye bowler's hande,
    Will let the balle go free.

And let ye middle stumpe be seen
    In line 'twixt him and you,
And in that very line I weene
    Will be your block so true.

Behinde ye crease your right foot place,
    All of the wicket cleare,
Your left leg forward throwe, and face
    Ye bowler without feare.

If your left shouldere you can see,
    And ye bowler's hande alsoe,
With a straight bat you'll surely bee
    All ready for the foe.

Keep that left shouldere up and wait,
  Watch where the ball doth bounde,
And on her put your bat full straight,
  And drive her on ye grounde.

Beware of balls that never rise,
  To play low doe not fail,
For shooters sinners doe surprise,
  They're like ye serpent's traile.

And if you thrive before you die
  Till a hundred years be past,
They'll say he ' scored a centurie,
  And his bails are off at last.'

Amen.
F. GALE.

Ballade of Dead Cricketers [1] ⚭ ⚭

Ah, where be Beldham now, and Brett,
  Barker and Hogsflesh, where be they?
Brett, of all bowlers fleetest yet
  That drove the bails in disarray?
And Small that would, like Orpheus, play
  Till wild bulls followed his minstrelsy? [2]
Booker, and Quiddington, and May?
  Beneath the daisies, there they lie!

And where is Lambert, that would get
  The stumps with balls that broke astray?
And Mann, whose balls would ricochet
  In almost an unholy way

---

[1] By permission of Messrs. Longmans, Green & Co.
[2] (So Nyren tells us.)

(So do ' baseballers ' pitch to-day) ;
  George Lear, that seldom let a bye,
And Richard Nyren, grave and grey ?
  Beneath the daisies, there they lie !

Tom Sueter, too, the ladies' pet,
  Brown that would bravest hearts affray ;
Walker, invincible when set,
  (Tom, of the spider limbs and splay) ;
Think ye that we could watch them, pray,
  These heroes of Broad-halfpenny,
With Buck to hit and Small to stay ?
  Beneath the daisies, there they lie !

ENVOY.

Prince, canst thou moralise the lay ?
  How all things change below the sky !
Of Fry and Grace shall mortals say,
  ' Beneath the daisies, there they lie ! '
ANDREW LANG.

An Over of Triolets [1]

I. CAUGHT !

I felt a flick below the wrist ;
So, grudgingly, I turned about :
Some red bird flitting by, I wist—
I felt a flick below the wrist—
Could Slip have caught it in his fist ?
The Umpire raised his hand. No doubt
I felt a flick below the wrist ;
So, grudgingly, I turned about.

[1] From *Cricket Poems*, by permission of the Author.

II. RUN OUT !

He did not linger on his way,
Nor stop to mark the Sun's decline;
More urgent need had he that day,
He did not linger on his way;
E'en when the Stumps about him lay—
Far scattered—ere he crossed the line,
He did not linger on his way,
Nor stop to mark the Sun's decline.

III. STUMPED !

You dared the joy of stepping out;
Take now the path that is the long one.
It seemed a simple Lob to clout.
You dared the joy of stepping out
And slogged, as if you had no doubt,
The very ball that was the wrong one—
You dared the joy of stepping out;
Take now the path that is the long one.

IV. BOWLED !

A half-remembered thing it came;
It broke discordant from the ground,
Like other balls, yet not the same—
A half-remembered thing it came.
There fell the shadow of a blame,
Dark herald of the coming sound—
A half-remembered thing it came,
It broke discordant from the ground.

V. MISSED !

A meteor, reeling through the air,
It was to him. ' No more,' quoth he.
'Twas hot and round and all aglare,
A meteor, reeling through the air,

That looked to come from everywhere,
And scored his fingers—and a three.
A meteor, reeling through the air,
It was to him.　'No more!' quoth he.

VI.　YORKED!

'Twas Summer when the Yorker sang;
Its sudden beauty haunts me still,
Through ether blue, red wonder sprang—
'Twas Summer when the Yorker sang—
I saw a rose—a star—a pang
Of light.　I heard the wickets thrill.
'Twas Summer when the Yorker sang;
Its sudden beauty haunts me still.
GEORGE FRANCIS WILSON.

Vitaï Lampada [1]

THERE'S a breathless hush in the Close to-night—
　Ten to make and the match to win—
A bumping pitch and a blinding light,
　An hour to play and the last man in.
And it's not for the sake of a ribboned coat
　Or the selfish hope of a season's fame,
But his captain's hand on his shoulder smote:
　'Play up! play up! and play the game!'

The sand of the desert is sodden red—
　Red with the wreck of a square that broke—
The Gatling's jammed and the Colonel dead,
　And the regiment blind with dust and smoke.

[1] From *Poems New and Old*, published by Mr. John
Murray, by permission of the Author.

The river of death has brimmed his banks,
  And England's far, and Honour a name,
But the voice of a schoolboy rallies the ranks :
  ' Play up ! play up ! and play the game ! '

This is the word that, year by year,
  While in her place the School is set,
Every one of her sons must hear,
  And none that hears it dare forget.
This they all with a joyful mind
  Bear through life like a torch in flame,
And falling, fling to the host behind—
  ' Play up ! play up ! and play the game ! '

                SIR HENRY NEWBOLT.

Shall I Never Storm or Swear ? [1]

SHALL I never storm or swear
Just because the umpire's fair ?
Or from expletives forbear,
'Cause he gives me out with care ?
Be he fairer, more upright
Than Carpenter or Lillywhite,
    If he will not favour me,
    What care I how fair he be ?

If ' How's that ? ' I loudly shout,
Let him promptly answer, ' Out ! '
If, perchance, I bowl a Wide,
Let him cough and look aside ;
If my toe slip o'er the crease,
Let him sigh, but hold his peace.
    If he cry ' No ball ! ' to me,
    What care I how fair he be ?

[1] By E. B. V. Christian, from *At the Sign of the Wicket,*
by permission of the Author.

When they catch me near the ground
Let him think 'twas on the bound ;
When against me they appeal
Let him hesitation feel ;
Let me profit by the doubt,
Let him never give me out.
        If ' leg-before ' he judges me,
        What care I how fair he be ?

' *Hobbs* '

THERE'S a little Cambridge man,
        Which is Hobbs,
And he's always in the van,
        Ain't yer, Hobbs ?
At the Oval or ' down under '
He seldom makes a blunder,
He's a champion little wonder
        Is our Hobbs !

You were born in '82,
        Weren't you, Hobbs ?
And you've made a tidy few
        Of runs since then, Master Hobbs.
He can bat and bowl and catch,
And in every cricket match
He's the best of all the batch,
        Ain't yer, Hobbs ?

So here's the best of luck
        To yer, Hobbs,
For we all admire your pluck,
        Don't we, Hobbs ?

You've put up a gallant fight,
And we think 'twould be but right
To see you made a knight,
        Sir J. B. Hobbs !
—W. M. in the *Evening News*, 1921.

' *Hobbs is Scoring To-day* '

(In respectful imitation of Mr. Austin Dobson).

HOBBS is scoring to-day :
Will he do so to-morrow ?
To see him in play
The crowd all will pay,
Altho' many may
Have a shilling to borrow.
Hobbs is scoring to-day :
Will he do so to-morrow ?
                MICHAEL SANTLEY.

A Cricket Romance

Two lovers went to the cricket game
    One afternoon. They say
He was a crank ; *she* never had seen
    Professional players play.

He faithfully tried to explain it all,
    She tried to understand ;
But the more he talked, the less she knew
    Why he thought the game was ' grand.'

He cheered, he danced, he yelled ' Hi ! hi ! '
    She calmly looked about,
And if anyone made a boundary hit,
    She asked if the man was ' out.'

She tried her best to keep the score,
 But when the game was done,
He found that, whenever a miss was hit,
 She had given the man a run.

It dampened his ardour to have her say :
 ' Why doesn't the umpire bat ? '
And each question she asked diminished his love,
 Though he wouldn't have owned to *that*.

Till at last she asked in a guileless way,
 ' Which eleven's playing now ? '
He broke the engagement then and there,
 And now they don't even bow !

A Match at Chislehurst, 1833 [1]   ◠

WHAT is all this noise about ?   And why this
 wondrous bustle ?
All the world comes out to see my noble Lord
 Charles Russell.
Good people ! do not run so fast, you should not
 act so rashly ;
For you can also take a peep at elegant H. Ashley.
  Yankee doodle, doodle doo, etc.

With Marsden, Pilch, and Cobbett too, I think it
 will be hard, oh !
If we don't rip the County up without the aid of
 Ward, oh !
' Aroint,' the Hampshire hero cries, ' Fell Aislabie,
 aroint, oh !
At least you will allow that I'm a *deep* one at the
 point, oh ! '

[1] The personal references are to noted players and
supporters of the game.

Marsden, Pilch, and Cobbett hit ; Hole puts the
    great pot on
At length the runs begin to flag, when in comes
    Vinny Cotton.
I've passed full many a pleasant day with gallant
    Captain Hawkins
But more with Willy Davison, whose *alias* was
    Dawkins.

Charles Lloyd he kissed the cook-maid in the
    sanctum where the books lie ;
Was this the tale the scullion told ?   Oh no ! it
    was the Cookes-ley.
It's many years since first my hair was cut and
    curled by John Brock,
But, though he cuts, he'll come again, my noble
    friend Lord Clonbrock.

There is a man at Chislehurst, of whose whole life
    the tenor
Is kindness and benevolence—Who's that—Sir
    Herbert Jenner !
He such a hearty welcome gives, and such a won-
    drous dinner,
That even if I lose the match, I still shall be a
    winner.

Herbert, the Phenomenon, is such a wondrous
    stumper,
So well bred a young gentleman—we'll toast him
    in a bumper :
Brother Charles is such a swell, and so is Alfred
    Mynn, Sir,
To entertain them *comme il faut* we'll go to the
    best inn, Sir.

Charley Harenc loves good wine, Charles loves good
    brandy,
Charley loves a pretty girl, as sweet as sugar candy ;
Charley is as sugar sweet, which wetted melts away,
    Sir,
Charley therefore stops away upon a rainy day, Sir.
Charley knocks the knuckles of many an awkward
    clown, Sir,
If Charley stops away again, he'll chance to rap
    his own, Sir.

Beldham Renovatus, re-cuscitatus Walker,
Hit so well, they put to silence Wodehouse the
    famed talker ;
All the world may take their leave, and go and
    live at Como,
Provided thither follow not any *nec vis neque homo.*

Lord Aboyne is just the same as when he was
    Strathavon,
If any make a match with him how closely they'll
    be shaven ;
In choosing a confederate, he wisely shows his sense,
    Sir,
By fixing on his liberal friend, the gallant Captain
    Spencer.

If you kill a little pig, mind that you do it scald
    well,
And if you want to run a rig, go lark it with George
    Caldwell ;
And if you wish to catch a bird, his tail you must
    put salt on,
If you angle for a fish, why, study Isaac Walton.

Dyke he leaves his troop and hounds—Dyke comes
    up to Town, Sir,
Dyke goes in at Marylebone—Dyke knocks his
    wicket down, Sir.

Fagge's the lad for me, my boys, tho' fagged I am
    for sartin,
And so I'll hang my hat up at the Tewkesbury
    Arms, John Martin.
' Finieram sat Telamon,' says Ovid and not Livy,
Should Chingford Churchyard be my lot, then I
    may say ' Finivi.'

                    BENJAMIN AISLABIE.

England, Past and Present   ∿   ∿

(After reading Nyren's *Young Cricketer's Tutor*)

  BUT for an hour to watch them play,
    Those heroes dead and gone,
  And pit our batsmen of to-day
    With those of Hambledon !
Our *Graces*, *Nyrens*, *Studds*, and *Wards*
    In weeks of sunny weather,
Somewhere upon Elysian swards,
    To see them matched together !

  Could we but see how *Small* withstands
    The three-foot break of Steel,
  If *Silver Billy's* ' wondrous hands '
    Survive with *Briggs* or *Peel !*
  If *Mann*, with all his pluck of yore,
    Can keep the leather rolling,
  And, at a crisis, notch a score
    When *Woods* and *Hearne* are bowling !

No doubt the *Doctor* would bewitch
   His quaint top-hatted foes,
Though, on a deftly chosen pitch,
   Old *Harris* bowled his slows ;
And *Aylward,* if the asphodel
   Had made the wicket bumpy,
Would force the game with *Attewell,*
   And *Stoddart* collar ' *Lumpy.*'

When Time of all our flannelled hosts
   Leaves only the renown,
Our cracks, perhaps, may join the ghosts
   That roam on Windmill Down,
Where shadowy crowds will watch the strife,
   And cheer the deeds of wonder
Achieved by giants whom in life
   A century kept asunder.

                              ALFRED COCHRANE.

The Fine Old English Cricketer   ↶

(*Air*—' The Fine Old English Gentleman ' or ' The
                  Highland Home.')

I'LL sing you a good old song, made to a good old
      rhyme,
Of a fine old English cricketer who loved his
      old pastime ;
Who deemed it nothing better than the very greatest
      crime
That cricket should be e'er forgot in any age or
      clime.
            Oh ! this fine old English cricketer, etc.

His house so old was hung around with bats and
    stumps and balls,
And many scores of games played out were placed
    against the walls,
And many books were laid about, in which with
    care he wrote
The names and style of playing of each cricketer of
    note.
        Oh ! this fine, etc.

When a winter's blast blew keenly past, this good
    old-fashioned soul
Would *bale* his goblet brimful from a rare old-
    fashioned *bowl* ;
He lov'd full well to sing or tell of some contested
    match ;
And oft would he declare with glee he ne'er had
    missed a *catch*.
        Oh ! this fine, etc.

And so it was when good old age, like snow, had
    blanched his hair,
That youthful heat yet warmed his heart—no cold-
    ness e'er dwelt there ;
And when at length his *stumps* gave way, yet still
    would he repair
The game to see, or umpire be, though seated in a
    chair.
        Oh ! this fine, etc.

But life's a game which all must play, and none
    can ever doubt
That though for years we may keep *in*, we must
    at length go *out*.

When eighty and ten notches full this rare old
    man had scored,
He fell. The rich and poor his loss most bitterly
    deplored.
       Oh ! this fine, etc.

The *bat* now flits o'er his remains—near yonder
    church they lie ;
Go—mark ! This simple epitaph will surely meet
    your eye :
' Here lies an honest cricketer, who never heaved
    a sigh,
Save when he found that some old friend had passed
    his *wicket* by.'
       Oh ! this fine, etc.

But tho' he's gone, yet still let us all imitate his
    ways—
Like him respected live and die, blest with each
    good man's praise.
Our good old games we'll cherish still, and prize
    them one and all,
And ' Cricket ne'er shall be forgot while we can
    play a ball.'
       Oh ! this fine, etc.

                  J. FFINCH.

Some other Poets   ∽   ∽   ∽

No authenticated paper has been discovered relative
to any hero in the game previous to 1719, when
Jenkins, in Thomas D'Urfey's *Pills to Pirge Melan-*

choly, appears to have been fairly bowled out by love. Here is the stanza referred to :

> His renown is fled and gone
> Since cruel Love pursued him
> Fair Winny's eyes bright shining
> And lily breast alluring
> Poor Jenkins' heart, with fatal dart,
> Her wounded past all curing.
> He was the prettiest fellow
> At football or at *cricket*.

Beyond such scraps as this, it seems remarkable that the old-time poets should have almost entirely ignored the game ; and indeed, cricket does not appear to have attracted much notice in comparison with other sports of a really trivial character, nearly all of which had their historians. Our great Shakespeare, above all others (as his writings abound with similes drawn from so many directions), one would have expected to have a deal to say ; but all the passages that I have been able to gather are, firstly the lines attributed to Soame Jenyns, who seemed, in his imitations of Horace, to have considered cricket ι very sporting amusement, for he writes :

England, when once at peace and wealth possest,
  Began to think frugality a jest,
So grew polite—hence all her well-bred heirs
  Gamesters and jockeys turn'd, and *cricket-players*—

Secondly, about the same time Alexander Pope's facetious lines :

> The Judge to dance his brother Sergeants call,
> The Senators at *cricket* urge the ball.

And thirdly, the words of Duncombe, who must have been wooing his muse near Canterbury when he wrote :

> An ill-timed *cricket match* there did
> At Bishopsbourne befall.

(Sir Horatio Mann, a great cricketer of his time, resided at Bourne Place, near here.) And in another place we find :

> We have not any *cricketer*
> Of such account as he.

In an old poem on cricket by James Love, a poet and comedian of London, written in 1744,[1] occur the following exhilarating lines :

> Hail, Cricket ! glorious, manly British game !
> First of all sports, be first alike in fame.

These lines are so oft quoted nowadays that it will interest many to know the source of their origin. Love used to write pieces for the great actor Garrick. Let me add :

> Stay, here's Kent, fertile in pheasants, cherries, hops, yeomen, codlings, and CRICKETERS.—Coleman the Younger.

W. W. READ.

---

[1] Reprinted 1770.

THE GAME IN FICTION

Tom Brown's Last Match ∽ ∽

(From *Tom Brown's School-days*, by THOMAS HUGHES)

TO-DAY the great event of the cricketing year, the Marylebone match, is being played. What a match it has been! The London eleven came down by an afternoon train yesterday, in time to see the end of the Wellesburn match ; and as soon as it was over, their leading men and umpire inspected the ground, criticizing it rather unmercifully. The Captain of the School eleven, and one or two others who had played the Lord's match before, and knew old Mr. Ainslabie and several of the Lord's men, accompanied them ; while the rest of the eleven looked on from under the Three Trees with admiring eyes, and asked one another the names of the illustrious strangers, and recounted how many runs each of them had made in the late matches in *Bell's Life*. They looked such hard-bitten, wiry, whiskered fellows that their young adversaries felt rather desponding as to the result of the morrow's match. The ground was at last chosen, and two men set to work upon it to water and roll ; and then, there being yet some half-hour of daylight, some one had suggested a dance on the turf. . . .

Deep had been the consultations at supper as to

the order of going in, who should bowl the first over,
whether it would be best to play steady or freely;
and the youngest hands declared that they shouldn't
be a bit nervous, and praised their opponents as the
jolliest fellows in the world, except perhaps, their old
friends the Wellesburn men.   How far a little good-
nature from their elders will go with the right sort
of boys !

The morning had dawned bright and warm, to the
intense relief of many an anxious youngster, up
betimes to mark the signs of the weather.   The
eleven went down in a body before breakfast, for a
plunge in the cold bath in a corner of the Close.
The ground was in splendid order, and soon after
ten o'clock, before spectators had arrived, all was
ready and two of the Lord's men took their places
at the wickets—the School, with the usual liberality
of young hands, having put their adversaries in
first.   Old Bailey stepped up to the wicket and
called ' play,' and the match had begun.

*   *   *   *   *

I wish I had space to describe the match ; how
the Captain stumped the next man off a leg-shooter,
and bowled small cobs to old Mr. Ainslabie, who
came in for the last wicket.   How the Lord's men
were out by half-past twelve o'clock for ninety-eight
runs.   How the Captain of the School eleven went
in first to give his men pluck, and scored twenty-five
in beautiful style ; how Rugby was only four
behind in the first innings.   What a glorious dinner
they had in the fourth-form school, and how the
cover-point hitter sang the most topping comic
songs, and old Mr. Ainslabie made the best speeches
that ever were heard, afterwards.   But I haven't

space, that's the fact, and so you must fancy it all,
and carry yourselves on to half-past seven o'clock,
when the School are again in, with five wickets
down and only thirty-two runs to make to win.
The Marylebone men played carelessly in their
second innings, but they are working like horses
now to save the match.

There is much healthy, hearty, happy life scattered
up and down the Close ; but the group to which I
beg to call your especial attention is there, on the
slope of the island which looks towards the cricket
ground.   It consists of three figures ; two are seated
on a bench, and one on the ground at their feet.
The first, a tall, slight, and rather gaunt man, with a
bushy eyebrow and a dry, humorous smile, is
evidently a clergyman. . . . And by his side, in
white flannel shirt and trousers, straw hat, the
Captain's belt, and the untanned yellow cricket
shoes which all the eleven wear, sits a strapping
figure near six feet high, with ruddy, tanned face
and whiskers, curly brown hair, and a laughing,
dancing eye.   He is leaning forward with his elbows
resting on his knees, and dandling his favourite bat,
with which he has made thirty or forty runs to-day,
in his strong brown hands.   It is Tom Brown,
grown into a young man nineteen years old, a
præposter and Captain of the eleven, spending his
last day as a Rugby boy, and let us hope as much
wiser as he is bigger, since we last had the pleasure
of coming across him.

And at their feet on the warm dry ground,
similarly dressed, sits Arthur, Turkish fashion, with
his bat across his knees.   He too is no longer a
boy, less of a boy in fact than Tom, if one may judge

from the thoughtfulness of his face, which is somewhat paler too than one could wish ; but his figure,
though slight, is well-knit and active, and all his old
timidity has disappeared, and is replaced by silent,
quaint fun, with which his face twinkles all over as
he listens to the broken talk between the other two,
in which he joins every now and then.

All three are watching the game eagerly, and
joining in the cheering which follows every good hit.
It is pleasing to see the easy, friendly footing which
the pupils are on with their master, perfectly
respectful, yet with no reserve and nothing forced
in their intercourse. Tom has clearly abandoned
the old theory of ' natural enemies,' in this case at
any rate. . . .

' Whose name is next on the list ? ' says the
Captain.

' Winter's, and then Arthur's,' answers the boy
who carries it ; ' but there are only twenty-six runs
to get, and no time to lose. I heard Mr. Ainslabie
say that the stumps must be drawn at a quarter-past
eight exactly.'

' Oh, do let the Swiper go in,' chorus the boys ;
so Tom yields against his better judgment.

' I dare say I've lost the match by this nonsense,'
he says as he sits down again ; ' they'll be sure to
get Jack's wicket in three or four minutes ; however,
you'll have the chance, sir, of seeing a hard hit or
two,' adds he, smiling and turning to the master.

' Come, none of your irony, Brown,' answers the
master. ' I'm beginning to understand the game
scientifically. What a noble game it is ! '

' Isn't it ? But it's more than a game. It's an
institution,' said Tom.

' Yes,' said Arthur, ' the birthright of British boys, old and young, as *habeas corpus* and trial by jury are of British men.'

' The discipline and reliance on one another which it teaches is so valuable, I think,' went on the master, ' it ought to be such an unselfish game. It merges the individual in the eleven ; he doesn't play that he may win, but that his side may.'

' That's very true,' said Tom, ' and that's why football and cricket, now one comes to think of it, are such much better games than fives or hare-and-hounds, or any others where the object is to come in first or to win for oneself, and not that one's side may win.'

' And then the Captain of the eleven ! ' said the master. ' What a post is his in our School-world ! Almost as hard as the Doctor's ; requiring skill and gentleness and firmness, and I know not what other rare qualities. . . .'

Meantime Jack Raggles, with his sleeves tucked up above his great brown elbows, scorning pads and gloves, has presented himself at the wicket ; and having run one for a forward drive of Johnson's, is about to receive his first ball. There are only twenty-four runs to make and four wickets to go down, a winning match if they play decently steady. The ball is a very swift one and rises fast, catching Jack on the outside of the thigh and bounding away, as if from india-rubber, while they run two for a leg-bye, amidst great applause and shouts from Jack's many admirers. The next ball is a beautifully-pitched ball for the outer stumps, which the reckless and unfeeling Jack catches hold of and hits right round to leg for five, while the applause becomes deafening ; only seventeen runs to get with four wickets—the game is all but ours !

It is ' over ' now, and Jack walks swaggering about his wicket with his bat over his shoulder, while Mr. Ainslabie holds a short parley with his men. Then the cover-point hitter, that cunning man, goes on to bowl slow twisters. Jack waves his hand triumphantly towards the tent, as much as to say, ' See if I don't finish it all off now in three hits.'

Alas, my son Jack ! the enemy is too old for thee. The first ball of the over Jack steps out and meets, swiping with all his force. If he had only allowed for the twist ! But he hasn't, and so the ball goes spinning up straight into the air as if it would never come down again. Away runs Jack, shouting and trusting to the chapter of accidents, but the bowler runs steadily under it, judging every spin, and calling out ' I have it ! ' catches it, and playfully pitches it on to the back of the stalwart Jack, who is departing with a rueful countenance.

' I knew how it would be,' says Tom, rising. ' Come along, the game's getting very serious.'

So they leave the island and go to the tent, and after deep consultation Arthur is sent in, and goes off to the wicket with a last exhortation from Tom to play steady and keep his bat straight. To the suggestions that Winter is the best bat left, Tom only replies, ' Arthur is the steadiest, and Johnson will make the runs if only the wicket is kept up.'

' I am surprised to see Arthur in the eleven,' said the master, as they stood together in front of the dense crowd which was now closing in round the ground.

' Well, I'm not quite sure that he ought to be in

for his play,' said Tom, ' but I couldn't help putting him in. It will do him so much good, and you can't think what I owe him.'

The master smiled. The clock strikes eight, and the whole field becomes fevered with excitement. Arthur, after two narrow escapes, scores one ; and Johnson gets the ball. The bowling and fielding are superb, and Johnson's batting worthy the occasion. He makes here a two and there a one, managing to keep the ball to himself, and Arthur backs up and runs perfectly ; only eleven runs to make now, and the crowd scarcely breathe. At last Arthur gets the ball again, and actually drives it forward for two, and feels prouder than when he got the three best prizes, at hearing Tom's shout of joy, ' Well played, well played, young 'un ! '

But the next ball is too much for a young hand, and his bails fly different ways. Nine runs to make and two wickets to go down—it is too much for human nerves !

Before Winter can get in, the omnibus which is to take the Lord's men to the train pulls up at the side of the Close, and Mr. Ainslebie and Tom consult, and give out that stumps will be drawn after the next over. And so ends the great match. Winter and Johnson carry out their bats, and, it being a one day's match, the Lord's men are declared the winners, they having scored the most in the first innings.

But such a defeat is a victory : so think Tom and all the School eleven, as they accompany their conquerors to the omnibus and send them off with three cheers, after Mr. Ainslebie has shaken hands all round, saying to Tom, ' I must compliment you, sir, on your eleven, and I hope we shall have you for a member if you come up to Town.'

How Dingley Dell played All-Muggleton

(From *The Pickwick Papers*, by Charles Dickens)

THE wickets were pitched, and so were a couple of marquees for the rest and refreshment of the contending parties. The game had not yet commenced. Two or three Dingley Dellers and All Muggletonians were amusing themselves with a majestic air by throwing the ball carelessly from hand to hand; and several other gentlemen dressed like them, in straw hats, flannel jackets, and white trousers—a costume in which they looked very much like amateur stonemasons — were sprinkled about the tents, towards one of which Mr. Wardle conducted the party.

Several dozen of ' How-are-you's ? ' hailed the old gentleman's arrival; and a general raising of the straw hats, and bending forward of the flannel jackets, followed his introduction of his guests as gentlemen from London who were extremely anxious to witness the proceedings of the day, with which, he had no doubt, they would be greatly delighted.

' You had better step into the marquee, I think, sir,' said one very stout gentleman, whose body and legs looked like half a gigantic roll of flannel elevated on a couple of inflated pillow-cases.

' You'll find it much pleasanter, sir,' urged another stout gentleman, who strongly resembled the other half of the roll of flannel aforesaid.

' You're very good,' said Mr. Pickwick.

' This way,' said the first speaker; ' they notch

in here—it's the best place in the whole field;' and the speaker, panting on before, preceded them to the tent.

'Capital game—smart sport—fine exercise—very,' were the words which fell upon Mr. Pickwick's ear as he entered the tent; and the first object that met his eyes was his green-coated friend of the Rochester coach, holding forth to the no small edification and delight of a select circle of the chosen of All-Muggleton. His dress was slightly improved and he wore boots; but there was no mistaking him.

The stranger recognized his friends immediately; and darting forth and seizing Mr. Pickwick by the hand, dragged him to a seat with his usual impetuosity, talking all the while as if the whole of the arrangements were under his especial patronage and direction.

'This way—this way—capital fun—lots of beer—hogsheads; rounds of beef—bullocks; mustard—cart-loads; glorious day—down with you—make yourself at home—glad to see you—very.'

Mr. Pickwick sat down as he was bid, and Mr. Winkle and Mr. Snodgrass also complied with the directions of their mysterious friend. Mr. Wardle looked on in silent wonder.

'Mr. Wardle—a friend of mine,' said Mr. Pickwick.

'Friend of yours!—My dear sir, how are you?—Friend of my friend's—give me your hand, sir'—and the stranger grasped Mr. Wardle's hand with all the fervour of a close intimacy of many years, and then stepped back a pace or two as if to take a full survey of his face and figure, and then shook

M

hands with him again—if possible—more warmly than before.

'Well; and how came you here?' said Mr. Pickwick, with a smile in which benevolence struggled with surprise.

'Come,' replied the stranger—'stopping at Crown—Crown at Muggleton—met a party—flannel jackets—white trousers—anchovy sandwiches—devilled kidneys—splendid fellows—glorious.'

Mr. Pickwick was sufficiently versed in the stranger's system of stenography to infer from this rapid and disjointed communication that he had, somehow or other, contracted an acquaintance with the All-Muggletons, which he had converted, by a process peculiar to himself, into that extent of good fellowship on which a general invitation may be easily founded. His curiosity was therefore satisfied, and putting on his spectacles, he prepared himself to watch the play which was just commencing.

All-Muggleton had the first innings, and the interest became intense when Mr. Dumkins and Mr. Podder, two of the most renowned members of that most distinguished club, walked, bat in hand, to their respective wickets. Mr. Luffey, the highest ornament of Dingley Dell, was pitched to bowl against the redoubtable Dumkins, and Mr. Struggles was selected to do the same kind office for the hitherto unconquered Podder. Several players were stationed to 'look out' in different parts of the field, and each fixed himself into the proper attitude by placing one hand on each knee, and stooping very much as if he were 'making a back' for some beginner at leap-frog. (All the regular players do this sort of thing—indeed, it's generally supposed that it is quite impossible to look out properly in any other position.)

The umpires were stationed behind the wickets ; the scorers were prepared to notch the runs ; a breathless silence ensued. Mr. Luffey retired a few paces behind the wicket of the passive Podder, and applied the ball to his right eye for several seconds. Dumkins confidently awaited its coming with his eyes fixed on the motions of Luffey.

'Play !' suddenly cried the bowler. The ball flew from his hand straight and swift towards the centre stump of the wicket. The wary Dumkins was on the alert ; it fell upon the tip of the bat and bounded far away over the heads of the scouts, who had just stooped low enough to let it fly over them.

'Run—run—another—Now then, throw her up —up with her—stop there—another—no—yes— no—throw her up, throw her up !' Such were the shouts which followed the stroke ; and, at the conclusion of which, All-Muggleton had scored two. Nor was Podder behindhand in earning laurels wherewith to garnish himself and Muggleton. He blocked the doubtful balls, missed the bad ones, took the good ones, and sent them flying to all parts of the field. The scouts were hot and tired, the bowlers were changed and bowled till their arms ached, but Dumkins and Podder remained unconquered. Did an elderly gentleman essay to stop the progress of the ball, it rolled between his legs or slipped between his fingers. Did a slim gentleman try to catch it, it struck him on the nose and bounded pleasantly off with redoubled violence, while the slim gentleman's eyes filled with water and his form

writhed with anguish. Was it thrown straight up
to the wicket, Dumkins had reached it before the
ball.

In short, when Dumkins was caught out and
Podder stumped out, All-Muggleton had notched
some fifty-four, while the score of the Dingley
Dellers was as blank as their faces. The advantage
was too great to be recovered. In vain did the
eager Luffey and the enthusiastic Struggles do all
that skill and experience could suggest to regain
the ground Dingley Dell had lost in the contest—
it was of no avail, and at an early period of the
winning game Dingley Dell gave in, and allowed the
superior prowess of All-Muggleton.

The stranger, meanwhile, had been eating,
drinking, and talking without cessation. At every
good stroke he expressed his satisfaction and ap-
proval of the player in a most condescending and
patronizing manner, which could not fail to have
been highly gratifying to the party concerned ;
while at every bad attempt at a catch, and every
failure to stop the ball, he launched his personal
displeasure at the head of the devoted individual
in such denunciations as ' Ah, ah ! stupid '—' Now,
butterfingers '—' Muff '—' Humbug '—and so forth
—ejaculations which seemed to establish him, in
the opinion of all around, as a most excellent and
undeniable judge of the whole art and mystery of
the noble game of cricket.

' Capital game—well played—some strokes admirable,' said the stranger, as both sides crowded
into the tent at the conclusion of the game.

' You have played it, sir ? ' inquired Mr. Wardle,
who had been much amused by his loquacity.

' Played it ! Think I have—thousands of times
—not here—West Indies—exciting thing—hot work
—very.'

' It must be rather a warm pursuit in such a
climate,' observed Mr. Pickwick.

' Warm !—red-hot—scorching—glowing. Played
a match once—single-wicket—friend the Colonel—
Sir Thomas Blazo—who should get the greatest
number of runs. Won the toss—first innings—
seven o'clock a.m.—six natives to look out—went
in ; kept in—heat intense—natives all fainted—
taken away—fresh half-dozen ordered—fainted
also—Blazo bowling—supported by two natives—
couldn't bowl me out—fainted too—cleared away
the Colonel—wouldn't give in—faithful attendant
—Quanko Samba—last man left—sun so hot bat
in blisters, ball scorched brown—five hundred and
seventy runs—rather exhausted—Quanko mus-
tered up last remaining strength—bowled me
out—had a bath, and went out to dinner.'

' And what became of what's-his-name, sir ? '
inquired an old gentleman.

' Blazo ? '

' No—the other gentleman ? '

' Quanko Samba ? '

' Yes, sir.'

' Poor Quanko—never recovered it—bowled on,
on my account—bowled off, on his own—died, sir.'
Here the stranger buried his countenance in a brown
jug, but whether to hide his emotion or imbibe its
contents, we cannot distinctly affirm.

The Cussedness of Cricket [1]   ᴐ   ᴐ

By J. C. Snaith.

' 'Mind taking the first ball, Halliday ? ' I said hoarsely.

' If you like,' said he ; then added, ' Just play your usual, and you're bound to get 'em.'

True cricketers are the soul of kindness.

Carefully noting at which end the wicket-keeper was, I just as carefully went to the one at which he was not. The mighty H. C. Trentham was just loosening his arm and sending down a few preliminaries. I watched him as keenly as the black mists before my eyes allowed. He brought his long brown arm right over with a beautiful, easy, automatic swing. The ball slipped from his fingers at an ordinary pace, but as soon as it took the ground it spun off the pitch with an inward twist at three times the rate one would expect. He looked every inch a bowler, powerfully built in every part.

However, the man preparing to resist him looked every inch a batsman too. Lithe, alert, calm, he seemed quietly happy that he had got to face a bowler worthy of his artifice. The manner in which he asked for guard, and took it, the elaborate process he went through to ensure the maintenance of ' two leg,' the diligent way in which he observed the placing of the field, and the freedom with which he ordered the screen about, all pointed to the conclusion that if Hickory got him out for fifty on that wicket they would be able to congratulate themselves. There is as much difference

---

[1] From *Willow the King*, by permission of the Author and of Ward, Lock & Co.

between a first-class cricketer and the ordinary club-man as there is between a professional actor and the gifted amateur. The club-man may be a marvel of conscientiousness, discretion, and enthusiasm, and able to recite Steel and Lyttelton from the preface to the index, but he has not that air of inevitableness that emphasizes the county man scoring off the best of Briggs and Richardson, and apparently able to compass any feat in the batting line but the losing of his wicket.

The terrific H. C. Trentham was now ready to deal destruction. Anxiously had I observed the placing of the field, the most noticeable items of which were the wicket-keeper standing a dozen yards behind the sticks, and the four men in the slips still deeper, with their hands on their thighs and their noses on a level with the bails. The bowler measured his distance, and scratched up the turf at his starting-place. The batsman set himself. The bowler walked a couple of yards, then broke into a trot, that gradually grew into a run, and when he arrived at the crease, with the velocity of a locomotive he hurled the ball from his hand, and his body after it, almost faster than the eye could follow. The captain fairly dug his bat into his block-hole, and the ball came back straight down the pitch, whizzing and rotating in half-circles. It was a most determined and barefaced attempt to ' york ' the captain, and the bowler smiled all over his countenance in a very winning manner.

The captain set himself again. The next ball was of a perfect length, a few inches on the off, and turned in suddenly with the ungenerous idea of hitting the top of the off-stump ; but the captain, watching it all the way, met it very warily, his right leg well against his bat, and blocked it gently back again to the bowler. The third had a very similar design, but happening to be pitched a little farther up, it came back as though propelled from a gun. The bowler neatly picked it up one hand, and drew the first cheer from the crowd. The fourth was full of guile. It was a trifle on the short side, wide of the off-stump, and instead of turning in was going away with the bowler's arm. The captain drew himself erect, held up his bat, and never made the least attempt to play it. The bowler smiled more winningly than ever. A London critic unburdened his mind by shouting, ' Nottingham ! ' The fifth was wickedness itself. The bowler covered his fifteen yards of run with exactly the same action and velocity, hurled down the ball with the same frantic effort of arms and body, but behold, the ball was as slow as possible, and the eye could distinctly follow it as it spun in the air with a palpable leg-bias. Even the great batsman who had to receive it was at fault. He played a little bit too soon, but, happily for Little Clumpton, the ground was so hard and true that it refused to take the full amount of work, and instead of its curling in and taking the captain's middle, as the bowler had intended, it refused to come in farther than the leg stick, which was conscientiously covered by the captain's pad. There it hit him, and rolled slowly towards the umpire, whilst the wicket-keeper pelted grotesquely after it.

' Come on ! ' I cried, seizing the opportunity, for I was very, very anxious for the captain to take first over from the other end. Accordingly we scuttled down the pitch, and I got home just as the wicket-keeper threw down my citadel.

' Well bowled, Charlie ! ' said the captain. But I think there was more in this than may appear, as I believe the thoughtful captain wished to attract my careful attention to that particular ball. Meantime the bowler had been grinning so violently at his own exceeding subtlety that mid-off politely requested him not to commit such an outrage on the handiwork of nature.

' Tom, you have a try that end,' said Captain George, throwing the ball to T. S. M. ' Set the field where you want 'em.'

' Left-hand round the wicket ! ' the umpire announced to the batsman ; ' covers 'em both, sir.' . . .

The Harrow boy began with a singular sort of movement that must have had a resemblance to the war-dance of the cheerful Sioux or the festive Shoshanee, which developed into a corkscrew kind of action that was very puzzling to watch, and imparted to the ball a peculiar and deceptive flight. He was quite slow, with a certain amount of spin and curl. The captain played right back to him every time, and, like the old Parliamentary hand he was, there was very little of the wicket to be seen, as his legs did their best to efface it. The captain had come in with the determination to take no liberties. He meant to play himself thoroughly well in before turning his attention to the secondary matter of making runs. If T. S. M. had been a Peate, his first over could not have been treated with a more flattering respect. The consequence was that he opened with a maiden also.

My turn had now arrived. I was called on to face the finest amateur bowler in England. Judging of the one over of his that I had had the privilege of witnessing, he appeared to combine the pace of a Kortright with the wiles of a Spofforth. Taking him altogether, he did not seem to be the nicest bowler in the world for a man of small experience and ordinary ability to oppose. But I remembered vaguely that the wicket was perfection, and that a straight bat would take a lot of beating. Besides, the black mists had lifted somewhat from my eyes, and the beastly funk had considerably decreased, as it often does when one is actually at work. All the same, I took my guard without knowing exactly what I did; I observed the field without knowing precisely how it was arranged, yet could see enough of it to be aware that point was looking particularly grim, and half inclined to chuckle, as though saying to himself, ' Oh, he's a young 'un, is he ? ' . . .

I planted my right foot on the edge of the crease with mathematical care, and set myself to meet the best bowler at either 'Varsity since Sammy Woods. My straining eyes never left him for an instant as he picked the ball up, worked his thumb up and down the seam, rubbed it on the ground, and then walked jauntily to his starting-point. I could see him all the way; the beautiful clear sunlight, the bright new red ball, and my own intentness almost enabled me to read the maker's name on the cover as he held it in his hand whilst he walked, trotted, galloped to the crease.

As he brought his arm high over his head, despite

the cessation of the screen's assistance, I could see the thumb and two fingers in which he grasped the ball, and every bit of his powerful wrist work. I had no time to think or to know where the ball was, however. But as it came humming from his hand instinct said, ' Go forward hard ! ' and forward I went, leg, bat, and elbow, for all that I was worth. There was a delicious vibration that told me the ball was timed to the second in the middle of the bat. It flew like a streak to mid-off all along the carpet ; but mid-off happened to be a county man, and it was back in the bowler's hands and threatening the captain's wicket just as ' No ! ' had left my mouth. And there was a personal compliment implied in the blinking eyes of H. C. Trentham and the benevolent smile of H. J. Halliday, that was a recompense for all the pains I was enduring and many hours of ' duck '-requited toil. I was conscious of an elated thrill running through my fibres as I awaited number two. Again I watched it eagerly as it came spinning through the sunlight and humming like a top ; again I could not say exactly where it was, but out went bat and leg and elbow, as before, and mid-off was afforded another opportunity for the exhibition of his skill. I set myself defiantly for number three. Let H. C. Trentham bowl his heart out. The third came along humming, and whizzing, and spinning, in the manner of the other two, but I had a vague sort of idea that it was a little wider and a little farther up. It was faster than an express train, but it merely appeared to delicately kiss the middle of the bat in the gentlest, sweetest way.

' Oh, well hit ! ' came the voice of the captain

down the wicket.   The crowd broke into a roar, and in a perfect ecstasy I looked into what I guessed should be the direction of the ball.   Behold! there was cover-point on the verge of the boundary waiting whilst a spectator officiously returned it. It was merely the force of habit that was responsible for that fourer, but the sensation of pure rapture was incomparable.   As there is nothing in the whole range of poetry or prose with which to point a parallel, it must be allowed that, beside a perfectly-timed boundary hit, on a hard ground from fast bowling, all other delights of this life are as nothingness.

The fourth ball came along in much the same way as the third, yet was appreciably shorter and slower.   I left it severely alone.   The fifth was a regular uprooting yorker, but I got my bat down in time and chopped it away.   So much for the crack's first over.   I had broken my duck in the most handsome manner—I could see the ball— I was beginning to be alarmingly happy—I never felt so fit and so much like making runs.   And I had only to continue as I had started to be sure of a trial for the county next week against Somerset. But I must restrain my eagerness, play steady, and keep cool.

The captain adopted the same tactics of masterly inactivity in regard to the second over of the youthful T. S. M.   He was quite an ordinary club-bowler compared to his great brother at the other end.   A shortish one was hooked quietly round to leg for a single, and it was my turn to meet him.   There was not a hint of my previous vacillation in the way I took my guard.   The buzzing in my head had altogether gone ; my eye was as clear and keen as possible. I had had my baptism of fire already. This was very common stuff—indeed, so much so that I took the liberty of turning the second ball I had of it to leg for three.

It being the last ball of the over, I had again to face H. C. With a bowler of his quality it requires a man of very great inexperience to be quite at ease or to think of attempting liberties. Therefore, again I concentrated the whole of my attention on every ball ; and the billiard-table pitch and a straight, unflinching bat enabled me to cope with his second over. It was a maiden, but it called for brilliancy on the part of mid-off, and a magnificent bit of fielding by Cateret in the slips, who saved a keen late cut from being a boundary, to make it one. Each ball was timed to the instant ; my wrists and the rare old blade with the wrapping at the bottom seemed to be endowed with magic ; the sun was just in the right place ; I had forgotten all about my cap, the screen, the might of the attack—forgot everything but the joy of achievement, so supreme was the sense of making runs with certainty and ease from county bowling, in the presence of an appreciative crowd on a great occasion. Here was Elysium. It was a sufficient recompense for a hundred failures. If I kept playing this game I couldn't but get 'em. Fifty was assured perhaps ; who knew—? But no man can be sanguine in regard to his first century—that is a bourn that few travellers ever reach.

The captain played T. S. M. gently for another single. I trotted down blithely to the other end. He was still bowling his slow leg-breaks, but it would be folly to attempt to drive him, as his flight was so deceptive ; besides, he had three men out. One ball which he delivered a full two yards behind the crease was tossed up so high that it was difficult to resist, as it appeared to be almost a half-volley at first sight. It actually dropped shorter than his others, however. This was the ball with which he usually got his wickets ; and although, crude as it was, it might do well enough for schoolboys, it was to be hoped that he didn't expect a man who intended to appear next week for his county to fall a victim to it ! If he did, he would very probably be disappointed.

The feel of that three to leg was still lingering in my wrist, and I was certain that this stroke could be played with impunity on this wicket. Besides, it would show the captain at the other end that I was by no means content to follow his lead, but had resources of my own. Again, if I persevered in getting T. S. M. away to leg, he would be certain to pitch them up a bit, and if he could only be persuaded to do this, sure as fate I should go out to him and lift him clear over the ring ! It wasn't such a very big hit ; besides, I felt capable of doing anything with ordinary club bowling. Really, I never felt so fit, and on such excellent terms with everybody and everything ! When I received the first ball of T. S. M.'s next over, I had a plan of the positions of the on-side fieldsmen in the corner of my eye. But it was such an excellent length that I had to play defensively. To my infinite pleasure, I immediately saw that the second was his usual shortish one. I promptly prepared to help myself to another three, stepped into my wicket so to do, but was so anxious to seize my opportunity that I had not troubled to note exactly how short it was. Therefore it rose a little higher than I expected, and I was also a little bit too soon. It hit me just above the pad with an almost caressing gentleness.

' How *was* that ? ' said the bowler, turning round to the umpire.

This didn't bother me in the least. I merely felt a trifle annoyed that my ardour had caused me to let off so bad a ball. But my pleasant meditations were suddenly disturbed by adjacent voices —' Chuckerrupp ! '

It never entered my head that I could be out by any possibility. The ball was a very vulgar long hop. I looked at the umpire with an air of bewilderment. He had a stolid solemnity that was funereal. I saw his hand go up. Thereon, with the blood buzzing in my ears, I made tracks for the pavilion. All the way I went I could not realize that I was out. My only sensation was the not unpleasing one of walking swiftly. Dead silence reigned as I marched in head down, thinking of nothing in particular. But the vision of the umpire's upthrown hand seemed to be painted on my retina.

The Ancient was in the dressing-room, brandishing his bat.

' Rough luck, old man ! ' he said.

Thereupon he went out to take my vacant place at the wicket, while I sat down, slowly mopped my wet face, rinsed my parched mouth, and then proceeded to take my pads off in the dullest, most apathetic manner.

George Meredith on Cricket   ✿   ✿

. . . Not one, but two men of Beckley—the last two—carried out their bats, cheered handsomely by both parties. The wickets pitched in the morning, they carried them in again, and plaudits renewed proved that their fame had not slumbered. To stand before a field—thoroughly aware that every successful stroke you make is adding to the hoards of applause in store for you—is a joy to your friends, an exasperation to your foes. I call this an exciting situation, and one as proud as a man may desire. Then, again, the two last men of an eleven are twins; they hold one life between them, so that he who dies extinguishes the other.

The sons of first-rate families are in the two elevens, mingled with the yeomen, and whoever can best do the business. Fallowfield and Beckley, without regard to rank, have drawn upon their muscle and science. One of the bold men of Beckley at the wickets is Nick Frim, son of the gamekeeper at Bickley Court; the other is young Tom Copping, son of Squire Copping, of Dox Hall, in the parish of Beckley. . . . The field was ringing at a stroke of Nick Frim's, who had lashed out in his old familiar style at last, and the heavens heard of it when Evan came into the circle of spectators. Nick and Tom were stretching from post to post, might and main. A splendid four was scored. The field took heart with the heroes; and presume not to doubt that heroes they are. It is good to win glory for your country; it is also good to win glory for your village.

EVAN HARRINGTON.

Cricket and Philosophy [1]   ⌒   ⌒

' THE instinct for games,' Wilhelmina remarked, ' is one which I never possessed. Let us see whether we can learn something.'

In obedience to her gesture, the horses were checked, and the footman clambered down and stood at their heads. Deyes, from his somewhat uncomfortable back seat in the victoria, leaned forward, and, adjusting his eyeglass, studied the scene with interest.

' Here,' he remarked, ' we have the " flannelled fool " upon his native heath. They are playing a game which my memory tells me is cricket. Every one seems very hot and very excited.'

Wilhelmina beckoned to the footman to come round to the side of the carriage.

' James,' she said, ' do you know what all this means ? '

She waved her hand towards the cricket pitch, the umpires with their white coats, the tent and the crowd of spectators. The man touched his hat.

' It is a cricket match, madam,' he answered, ' between Thorpe and Nesborough.'

Wilhelmina looked once more towards the field, and recognized Mr. Hurd upon his stout little cob.

' Go and tell Mr. Hurd to come and speak to me,' she ordered.

The man hastened off. Mr. Hurd had not once turned his head. His eyes were riveted upon the

[1] From *The Missioner*, by E. Phillips Oppenheim, by permission of the Author.

game. The groom found it necessary to touch him on the arm before he could attract his attention. Even when he had delivered the message, the agent waited until the finish of the over before he moved. Then he cantered his pony up to the waiting carriage. Wilhelmina greeted him graciously.

'I want to know about the cricket match, Mr. Hurd,' she asked, smiling.

Mr. Hurd wheeled his pony round so that he could still watch the game.

'I am afraid that we are going to be beaten, madam,' he said dolefully. 'Nesborough made 198, and we have six wickets down for fifty.'

Wilhelmina seemed scarcely to realize the tragedy which his words unfolded.

'I suppose they are the stronger team, aren't they?' she remarked. 'They ought to be. Nesborough is quite a large town.'

'We have beaten them regularly until the last two years,' Mr. Hurd answered. 'We should beat them now but for their fast bowler, Mills. I don't know how it is, but our men will not stand up to him.'

'Perhaps they are afraid of being hurt,' Wilhelmina suggested innocently. 'If that is he bowling now, I'm sure I don't wonder at it.'

Mr. Hurd frowned.

'We don't have men in the eleven who are afraid of getting hurt,' he remarked stiffly.

A shout of dismay from the onlookers, a smothered exclamation from Mr. Hurd, and a man was seen on his way to the pavilion. His wickets were spread-eagled, and the ball was being tossed about the field.

'Another wicket!' the agent exclaimed testily.
'Crooks played all round that ball!'

'Isn't that your son going in, Mr. Hurd?' Wilhelmina asked.

'Yes! Stephen is in now,' his father answered.
'If he gets out, the match is over.'

'Who is the other batsman?' Deyes asked.

'Antill, the second bailiff,' Mr. Hurd answered.
'He's captain, and he can stay in all day, but he can't make runs.'

They all leaned forward to witness the continuation of the match. Stephen Hurd's career was brief and inglorious. He took guard and looked carefully round the field with the air of a man who is going to give trouble. Then he saw the victoria, with its vision of parasols and fluttering laces, and the sight was fatal to him. He slogged wildly at the first ball, missed it, and paid the penalty. The lady in the carriage frowned, and Mr. Hurd muttered something under his breath as he watched his son on the way back to the tent.

'I'm afraid it's all up with us now,' he remarked.
'We have only three more men to go in.'

'Then we are going to be beaten,' Wilhelmina remarked.

'I'm afraid so,' Mr. Hurd assented gloomily.

The next batsman had issued from the tent and was on his way to the wicket. Wilhelmina, who had been about to give an order to the footman, watched him curiously.

'Who is that going in?' she asked abruptly.

Mr. Hurd was looking not altogether comfortable

'It is the young man who wanted to preach,' he answered.

Wilhelmina frowned.

'Why is he playing?' she asked. 'He has nothing to do with Thorpe.'

'He came down to see them practise a few evenings ago, and Antill asked him,' the agent answered. 'If I had known earlier I would have stopped it.'

Wilhelmina did not immediately reply. She was watching the young man who now stood at the wicket, bat in hand. In his flannels he seemed a very different person from the missioner whose request a few days ago had so much offended her. Nevertheless, her lip curled as she saw the terrible Mills prepare to deliver his first ball.

'That sort of person,' she remarked, 'is scarcely likely to be much good at games. Oh!'

Her exclamation was repeated in various forms from all over the field. Macheson had hit his first ball high over their heads, and a storm of applause broke from the bystanders. The batsman made no attempt to run.

'What is that?' Wilhelmina asked.

'A boundary—magnificent drive,' Mr. Hurd answered, excitedly. 'By Jove, another!'

The agent dropped his reins and led the applause. Along the ground this time, the ball had come at such a pace that the fieldsman made a very half-hearted attempt to stop it. It passed the horses' feet by only a few yards. The coachman turned round and touched his hat.

'Shall I move farther back, madam?' he asked.

'Stay where you are,' Wilhelmina answered. shortly. Her eyes were fixed upon the tall, lithe figure once more facing the bowler. The next ball was the last of the over. Macheson played it carefully for a single, and stood prepared for the bowling at the other end. He began by a graceful cut or two, and followed it up by a square-leg hit clean out of the ground. For the next half an hour the Thorpe villagers thoroughly enjoyed themselves. Never since the days of one Foulds, a former blacksmith, had they seen such an exhibition of hurricane hitting. The fast bowler, knocked clean off his length, became wild and erratic. Once he only missed Macheson's head by an inch, but his next ball was driven fair and square out of the ground for six. The applause became frantic.

Wilhelmina was leaning back amongst the cushions of her carriage, watching the game through half-closed eyes, and with some apparent return of her usual graceful languor. Nevertheless, she remained there, and her eyes seldom wandered for a moment from the scene of play. Beneath her apparent indifference, she was watching this young man with an interest for which she would have found it hard to account, and which instinct alone prompted her to conceal. It was a very ordinary scene, after all, of which he was the dominant figure. She had seen so much of life on a larger scale—of men playing heroic parts in the limelight of a stage as mighty as this was insignificant. Yet, without stopping to reason about it, she was conscious of a curious sense of pleasure in watching the doings of this forceful young giant. With an easy good-humoured smile, replaced every now and then with a grim look of determination as he jumped out from the crease to hit, he continued his victorious career, until a more frantic burst of applause than usual announced that the match was won.

'RANJI'

C. B. Fry's Estimate ⌢ ⌢ ⌢

HE does nothing blindly. He thinks about the game, starts a theory, and proceeds to find out what use it is. Some of his strokes were discovered by accident. For instance, his inimitable leg-play began thus: When a boy, he started with the usual fault of running away from every fast ball that threatened to hit him. But, instead of edging off towards square-leg as most boys do, he used, with characteristic originality, to slip across the wicket towards point. Suddenly he found that by moving the left leg across towards the off, keeping his bat on the leg side of it, and facing the ball quite squarely with his body, he could watch the ball on the bat and play it away to leg with a twist of the wrist.

His forward play is somewhat unorthodox, as he walks out to the ball when he hits, but it is none the less strong and safe. He can drive finely in all directions when in the mood—indeed, at his best he can use every stroke ᐧin the game. He is a beautiful field in any position. He excels at point or in the slips, where there is scope for his quickness; but as he can pick up a ball very clean, catch any-thing, and throw well, he is almost equally good

as extra-cover or in the long-field ; and he rarely
goes on to bowl without getting a wicket or having
a catch missed off him.

Eight Rules for Fieldsmen ∽ ∽

ALWAYS back up the man who is receiving the
ball at the wicket, when it is thrown in, but not
too close.

Always try for a catch, however impossible it
may seem.

Always be on the look-out and ready to start.

Run at top speed, but not rashly, the moment
the ball is hit.

Use both hands whenever possible.

Do not get nervous if you make a mistake.

Obey your captain cheerfully and promptly.

Never be slack about taking up the exact position
assigned to you ; never move about in an aimless,
fidgety manner.

K. S. RANJITSINHJI.

On Wider Wickets ∽ ∽ ∽

SOME years ago, when a controversy on the subject
of affording some assistance to the bowlers was in
progress, one of the most famous cricketers of our
time made a remark which has always remained
in my memory. ' Whatever changes are made
by the authorities of the game,' wrote the Hon.
F. S. Jackson, ' I hope that no interference with
the implements of cricket is contemplated.' I
cordially agreed with Mr. Jackson's view at that
time, and I have seen no cause to alter my opinion
since.

As far as I am aware, the dissatisfaction as to drawn games refers principally to first-class cricket. It would be highly injurious, therefore, to alter the existing state of things in order to remedy an evil which exists only in the highest class of cricket, provided we admit that there is an evil due, primarily and absolutely, to the ascendancy of the bat. First-class matches form but a small proportion of the world's cricket, however important an item it may be. It would be very injurious to sacrifice the interests of the rest of the community—even for the sake of an important minority—thereby introducing, to employ a political phrase, class legislation. The game, whether it is called first-class or otherwise, is CRICKET, and any measure can only be a half-measure which aims at differentiating between the classes of cricket.

The great radical change—for it is reasonable to suppose that when wickets are sufficiently wide all matches will be finished within the prescribed period—will deprive the game of its greatest charm of uncertainty, a consummation which, I feel sure, is not desired by true lovers of the game all over the world.

K. S. RANJITSINHJI.

On Captaincy ⌁ ⌁ ⌁ ⌁

THE captain creates the moral atmosphere of his side. If he is slack and indifferent, so are the other ten; if he is keen and enthusiastic, so are they. Unconsciously, the side as a whole assumes the captain's attitude towards cricket and towards a particular match. So his duties in the field involve a good deal besides the actual management of bowling and the arrangement of fieldsmen. If his side is to play the game in the right spirit and the spirit that wins matches, he must be kind, cheerful, and enthusiastic, and must always try his best. It is impossible to give advice on such points. The only thing is for a captain to realize what it is that is required, and to see the importance of fulfilling this to the utmost of his ability.

On Australian Cricket

I CANNOT help thinking that a little too much importance is attached to the result of figures in Australia, and it is sometimes the cause of the interest of the side being made subservient to the interests of the player. A few years ago in England, much of the individual interest was exhibited for certain players who played more for their average than for the interest of their side, on purpose to win a trophy given by a certain newspaper each month to the player having the best average. Fortunately for the game, this has been discontinued.

English bowlers who go out to Australia, unless they are naturally gifted bowlers, find that, owing to the glossy surface of the pitches and the pace with which the balls rebound, they are at sea. The wicket lasts considerably longer than is necessary for the completion of the match in most instances, and they find that the patience of the Australian batsmen is untiring, and that their length, upon which they mainly depend, is not in itself sufficient to get wickets; so that the fire of their bowling gradually wears out, and they gradually weaken their attack. Then they bowl like machines, and are at the mercy of the batsmen. From these remarks it will naturally follow that English players stand a better chance against Australian combinations on slow, sticky pitches.

On Coaching   ⌒   ⌒   ⌒   ⌒

MUCH may be done in the way of self-coaching. A boy should always remember, when practising without his coach, those points to which his attention has been called. Some authorities think there is great virtue in practising strokes and positions without a ball or bowler. It can be done in the bedroom, in fact. The idea is, that such practice gets the body used to the movements required on the field, so that when the strokes are tried in games the necessary positions are more readily assumed. I have never tried this kind of practice myself, but there is certainly no harm in it. Looking-glasses and wash-hand basins are the only things likely to suffer by bedroom practice. The great Harry Jupp is said to have practised daily in front of a looking-glass in order to make sure of playing with a straight bat. He had a chalk line on the floor, and used to swing his bat up and down it. At any rate, such practice shows a proper feeling about the game. No stone should be left unturned in order to improve and develop one's batting. It must be remembered that a great amount of labour, and even drudgery, is required before a man can become a really good player. The greater and more consistent the effort after improvement, the sooner will a fair

degree of skill be acquired. At the same time,
playing cricket ought not to be turned into a
weariness of the flesh. Boys should be taught to
work at it, but they should also be taught to love
it.

A Philadelphian Estimate   ⌒   ⌒

LIST ye, thou well-dressed dweller in the town,
what a Prince effects on Sunday evening in Philadelphia. He wore a soft flannel pink-striped
shirt, dark cheviot suit, russet shoes, a tie that was
red, green, yellow, and purple, and looked like a
rainbow with chronic convulsions, a soft slouch
hat with a ribbon around it that was mostly yellow,
but had six or seven other shy colours to it—and
his cuffs are apparent by reason of their lack.
' What's the use of being a dude ? ' asked
Ranji. ' No one can be a dude and anything else
at the same time—and I'd rather be anything
else than a dude.' Which sentence proves that
Ranji's wit is as nimble as the convulsive colours
of his Sunday's tie. ' Funny, isn't it ? ' asked
Ranji, as he lit a big black cigar. ' Going out to
one of your ball games this week, and I'm going
to root. I caught that word " root " this morning,
and it's all right. A man told me that a pig roots,
and that it turns up things that never would turn
up if it wasn't rooted for. And so if a team isn't
winning, and you don't expect it to turn up on top,
why you've got to root for it. Then if you root
hard enough, why, you turn up a victory when it
wasn't looked for. And then if you root every
day the people call you a rooter, and they think
you're a jolly good fellow because you don't lose

heart, you know, but just keep on rooting until you bring things on top. And so I'm going out to see some of your ball games, and I'm going to " root " because I like the spirit of the thing, you know—and I like the word too !'

A great fellow is ' Ranji '—a thoroughbred, a masculine winner—chock-full of a big wholesome personality—brimming over with good, healthy, contagious enthusiasm. He's as democratic in his way as a messenger-boy—as free from foppery and affectation as a bootblack. But, best of all— and hearken, all ye Quaker maids—he's thirty-eight [1] and single !

[1] [He was just twenty-seven and a non-smoker.]

ENGLAND v. AUSTRALIA

The Origin of 'The Ashes'

IN AFFECTIONATE REMEMBRANCE

OF

ENGLISH CRICKET,

WHICH DIED AT THE OVAL

ON

29th August, 1882.

Deeply lamented by a large circle of
sorrowing friends and acquaintances.

R.I.P.

N.B.—The body will be cremated, and the
ashes taken to Australia.

A Welcome to the English Eleven, 1879

WE welcome all and each with open hearts—
  Lord Harris, Hornby, Lucas, Webbe, and Hone;
Who with the rest will bravely do their parts
  To shine with us as formerly they've shone
On other fields. We gladly would atone
  For past defeats by triumphing o'er you;
Still, should we fail, we'll neither fret nor moan,

191

But take our beating as brave warriors do—
When fortune smites them down, they ever climb
   anew.

An Imaginary Reception to the English Eleven, 1879 ◠   ◠   ◠   ◠

LORD HARRIS and Gentlemen Cricketers of England,
you do me proud.   You'd better believe I'm mighty
glad to see you, and congratulate you upon having
stirred your stumps as far as the fair city of Adelaide.
As Mr. Coglin would say, I'll go *bail* you won't
regret going so far *a-field*.   I am here, gentlemen,
surrounded by my councillors, in the multitude of
whom I do assure you there is wisdom, though perhaps you might not think it to look at 'em.   (Here
his worship pushed Councillors Raphael and Hol-
land to the front, and Lord Harris and his men
gazed on them with wonder and admiration in
their looks.)   If our cricketers are not exactly
Graces, our councillors are.   (Hear, hear.)   Yet,
gentlemen, our men are not the minutest of tubers,
and after you have *Harrised* them a bit ('Oh!') they
may *worry* through somehow.   I fear we shall not
be able to provide you with a nice Christian young
man who will play with your watch while you bat
or field, but you will find many who will watch
your play.   Our Australian team in America found
the thing work the other way.   Our cricketers
will try to prove foemen worthy of your *Steel*,
or rather your willow, but won't steal your watch,
though they *will owe* you something when you
leave.   ('Oh, oh!' and cheers.)   You will, I'm sure,
receive every attention from the inhabitants of

Adelaide, particularly from our mosquitoes, who are always *pressing* in their attentions and their proboscis when they meet new arrivals.

England v. Australia ᴐ ᴐ ᴐ

WELL done, Cornstalks ! Whipt us
    Fair and square.
Was it luck that tript us ?
    Was it scare ?
Kangaroo Land's ' Demon,' or our own
Want of ' devil,' coolness, nerve, backbone ?

Ivo Bligh [1] ᴐ ᴐ ᴐ ᴐ

(*Air*—' Nelly Bly.')

Ivo BLIGH had a shy
    At Australian sticks ;
Scored like fun, gave them one
    Of the neatest licks.
Hi Ivo ! Ho Ivo !
    Britons breathe once more,
Whilst they fill to your skill
    And Leslie's spanking score !
Ivo Bligh, England's eye
    Murdoch fairly wiped ;
Leslie's ' gross ' retrieves our loss.
    How he must have swiped !
Hi Ivo ! Ho Ivo !
    Stick to it !—you *will*.
Not for ' crow,' just to show
    England's ' in it ' still.

[1] The Earl of Darnley, leader of the English Team to Australia, 1882–3.

' *Lucky Warner* '

THE first match of a tour is always an anxious one, especially for a captain.   Everything is so different, —conditions, light, wicket, and a good start mean so much.   They used before this tour to call me ' Lucky Warner ! ' and when I went out to toss with Hill, a man in the ring cried out, ' What's the use of tossing with Lucky Warner, Clem ? ' and when I won, he added, ' Of course he won, Clem. Lucky Warner—told you so.'

P. F. WARNER.

Australian   Wickets

EVERYBODY knows that in the two countries the seasons differ, and that when football reigns in the one Cricket is king in the other.   Football is the most popular game in Australia, but cricket is the national game of the Colonies, and throughout the winter there are hundreds and thousands of Australians who, although there is no cricket for them to see, eagerly watch for the newspapers which contain the accounts of English matches.

The regulation season begins in October and terminates in April ; but the game might be played all the year round in some parts of Australia— in the arid interior, for instance, where the annual rainfall averages anything from one to five or six inches, where rain may not fall for months, and even when it does the greater portion of the year's average is shed by one thunderstorm.   As a matter of fact, cricket is going on in some parts of the vast

Austral continent in every month of the year, for many farmers who in October begin to reap their hay crops (after which they have to take in the harvest of golden grain), play during the winter, which they are able to do on their hard earth or asphalt wickets. I have heard of games being played on the dry salt-pans in some parts of Australia. These are nothing less than the beds of shallow lakes or lagoons, which a long spell of drought has dried up. The wicket while it lasts is beautifully level, but it quickly cuts up, and the stumps have now and again to be moved a few feet.

In Sydney and Melbourne, the largest centres of population, there is too much rain for cricket to be comfortably played on turf wickets throughout the winter ; but in Adelaide, the capital city of South Australia, the winter is milder, and on the Adelaide Oval, if cricketers were so inclined, the game might be indulged in all the year round, without any more inconvenience than English players suffer from the wet in an average English summer ! I am sure that in Adelaide we rarely have a winter during which more rain falls than the Australian Eleven of 1882 experienced during an English summer. The average rainfall for the whole year in Adelaide is no more than about 20 inches ! It would not, however, do for all cricketers to play cricket constantly, for the one important reason, if for no other, that they would become stale.

It is upon what are known as matting wickets, and entirely without coaching, that the average Australian cricketer learns the rudiments of the game ; and when this is considered the standard

o

of excellence to which Australians have attained is
the more remarkable. In England your village
lads, your schoolboys, and your University men
are accustomed to grass wickets from their earliest
days, so that when promotion comes to a high-class
eleven they have the advantage of having been
grounded in the rudiments of the game under
conditions similar to those which rule on the more
important battling grounds. But in Australia
much that has been learnt by the lad on matting
wickets has to be forgotten when he is promoted
to one of the few clubs which play on turf
pitches.

GEORGE GIFFEN.

The Eleventh Australian Eleven ⌒

DOES your circulation fail,
            Kangaroo?
Got a frost-bite in your tail,
            Kangaroo?
Do you find it hard to play
When it's hailing half the day,
And it's even cold for May,
            Kangaroo?

Are your Noble, Duff, and Hill,
            Kangaroo?
And poor Trumper feeling ill,
            Kangaroo?
Has the voyage made them stale,
Since Llewellyn did not fail
When he started ' finding bail,'
            Kangaroo?

'Tis no doubt a sudden change,
            Kangaroo ;
But you'd sooner find your range,
            Kangaroo,
If in coming o'er the seas,
In the chambers where they freeze,
You were hardened by degrees,
            Kangaroo !

A. O. Jones on Australian Bowling

THE Australian is far ahead of us in bowling.
Why is it ? Because on the perfect wickets out
there it would be impossible for him to get any
batsman out unless he made the ball do something.
Watch an Australian bowler : he is always doing
something to the ball with his fingers, and never
bowls a ball down unless he has some object in
view. I think perhaps the best instance of an
Australian bowler, and our Englishmen know him
best—and that is why I take him as an example
—is Albert Trott. He holds the ball in the most
extraordinary way ; in fact, sometimes you would
think it would be impossible for him to get rid of
it. Another great thing in his favour is that he is
always willing to ' speculate.'

' Barracking' in Australia

WHEN we were at Melbourne the ' barrackers'
were in fine form. Somehow, I love these ' barrackers.' They are generally so full of humour, and
they do know something about the game.
    Mr. Douglas was bowling with his back to the
scoring board (only one was working), and his

analysis (which is always shown on Australian scoring boards) read no wickets for some 60 runs. Then somebody shouted, ' Why didn't you go on at the other end, Johnny ? You would then see your analysis.'

During the second innings of the same match Wilfred Rhodes was bowling, and had already secured two or three wickets when Douglas went into the long-field to Woolley, who was the bowler at the other end. A man in the crowd called out, suddenly, ' Here you, Johnny ; Rhodes has been bowling for an hour and twenty minutes. Why don't you take the poor old man off ? ' Wilfred finished up with six wickets for some 30 runs. What a great bowler he is to be sure !

J. B. HOBBS.

The M.C.C. Dinner at Sydney (Feb. 27, 1912) ❧ ❧ ❧ ❧ ❧

MENU

' On a good wicket.'

HEARNE BAY OYSTER COCKTAILS
' First wicket down.'

TURTLE SOUP AU DOUGLAS (slow but sure)
' How's that ? '

RHODES SCHNAPPER À LA CENTURY
' Going great Gun(n)s.'

FOSTER-ED BARN(ES) CHICKEN AU MAIDEN
' Clean bowled.'

CHAMPAGNE PUNCH À LA CAMPBELL
' All out to Pommery 04.'

SADDLE WOOLLEY LAMB AND VINE SAUCE
' *Still no Hitch.*'

HOBB-LED ASPARAGUS AND PASLEY DRESSING.
' *Another boundary.*'

PECHE WARNER
' *Plums out of Season.*'

SMITH BEHIND MARYLEBONE STUMPS
' *Ashes on Toast.*'

The Rage for Rot ᴓ   ᴓ   ᴓ   ᴓ

(From the *Sydney Bulletin*, 1912.)

[J. W. H. T. Douglas fields without his hat in all weathers.
The English skipper is said to be immune from sunstroke.

Hobbs, in addition to being a stylish bat and an eloquent
writer of the English language, is one of the finest draughts
players in his native town.

The best-dressed man in the team is undoubtedly
Foster—A London fashion-leader is reported to have
said : ' See Foster's trousers and die.'—*News Drivel.*]

You know where William Biffkins fields,
When Bloggs, ' the Terror,' bowls ;
You've learned the brand of hat which shields
The skull of ' Slogger ' Coles.
Do not desist,
Go on, persist
In piling up your score
Of yarns old, new,
Absurd, false, true—
The sum of cricket lore.

How good it is to know that Gunn
Wears Jaegar underwear,
That Douglas braves our tropic sun
In nothing but his hair,
That Smiter drinks,
And Bliter winks
At ev'ry girl he sees !
What interest
And added zest
One gets from facts like these !

The flannel pants of Foster cost
A guinea clear per pair.
Hearne's work out rather less. Hobbs lost
A tenner once—a rare
Experience
With him, his sense
Of caution being strong
And, *à propos*,
It riled him so,
He cursed both loud and long.

Such is the news the public race
To purchase day by day ;
In truth one may, without a trace
Of overstatement say :
That rot like this
Affords more bliss
Than anything to some,
A fact, alas !
Which shows the pass
To which our 'sports' have come.

AUGUSTUS BAILS.

IN OTHER CLIMES

A Cricket Tour in India : The Passage Out ⟳ ⟳ ⟳ ⟳

A CRICKET tour may seem a simple thing to manage, but it is not merely a matter of saying to one cricketer after another, Come, and he cometh. Few people would believe, unless they went into the question thoroughly, how enormous is the amount of detail which has to be arranged for a trip of this kind, and it is upon the skill and foresight of the manager that the success of the trip from the point of view of those who participate in it depends. Tickets, customs, luggage, and the painting of it, clothes suitable for all purposes and all temperatures, the matter of hats and hospitality, and the very serious questions of servants and washing ; these in addition to a thousand other minor things must all be thought of and provided for.

Our start was most auspicious. The pitch rolled out well—I mean the ship did not pitch, and the rollers did not roll. Never have I seen the Channel and the Bay more charming. Sunny, smooth, and warm without being foggy this voyage offered a striking contrast to the last time I had made it, some few months before, in a small ' tramp ' which for twenty-four hours had only been able to make

one knot an hour in the teeth of a gale, and had
taken over a fortnight to reach Lisbon.   Calm as
it was, however, the motion of the ship proved too
much for many, and for the first few days the team
was distinctly *piano*.·   In a row of uniform chairs
they lay disconsolately gazing over the waste of
waters, wondering no doubt why they had been so
foolish as to come.   The deck-steward could not
charm them to games of bull or quoits, charmed he
never so wisely ; all the wealth of English woman-
hood on board left them cold as yet and unconcerned.
But in a few days there was a revival, and deck-
cricket took place in the Bay itself.

Thereafter a choppy sea, and the tail of a storm
in the Gulf of Lyons.   The lions roared—and if
they suffered hunger, it was not altogether our
fault, Stromboli in eruption, the Straits of Messina
and Bonifacio ; then the rocky shores of Crete,
shining above us through a haze of amethyst hue,
and hiding from our ken the Labyrinth of the
Minotaur—that minotaur whom Mr. Evans has so
unkindly exploded, proving once more the futility
of learning history which always promotes the
unknowing of the known.   For the oldest historical
fact is always being subverted by the newest
historical theory, as the late Lord Lytton used to
complain. Next Port Said, ugly as ever, but
nowadays a comparatively virtuous port, and after
the abominable process of coaling we entered the
Suez Canal, that modern product of French genius
and English practical ability. Percival Landon,
talker, herald, journalist, was on board. We had
renewed our Oxford friendship, and I remember
we sat and talked of the canal, of its ancient and

romantic history, of Herodotus and the Pharaohs, of Gaul and Britain, of America and Panama, till the canal seemed to be the very pivot of the universe, the greatest of ancient facts, the finest of modern achievements, more wonderful than the Nile, and yet more marvellous than ocean.

There is little that is modern in the fact of the canal itself. Did not Pharaoh Necho construct one hereabouts (600 B.C.), and did not the old historian, Herodotus, describe for us his journey down it ? What is new is the puffing, busy little train and the vast steamers with their smoking funnels. But they hardly seem realities. An hour passes, and for the Arab on his camel nothing is left of these save a stretch of black cloud in the sky. Only the desert remains, and the eternal silence, the boundless vista, and the passing mirage. Can you wonder if the West, with all its works, its noise, and steam, and engines, seems here a mirage also—a phantom appearing and disappearing on the horizon —whilst the East with its deep worn ways is the reality that abides ? . . .

I have dealt elsewhere with the growing enthusiasm of the natives of India for cricket, an enthusiasm which, if it continues to increase, will, in my opinion, soon result in producing quite first-class teams among them. There are many fine cricketers in India to-day, born to bat unknown till they are revealed to larger public by the visit of an English team like K. J. Key's eleven.

The potent, if lamentable, fact is that men do not keep up their cricket out here as they used to do. On all sides you hear the same lament, and if you begin to search for reasons, several present themselves to you. It is urged, in general, that for Europeans cricket is not a game best suited to the conditions of modern India. It is, to begin with, too long a game. You want, in India, a game which is both violent and short. You do not want a game which keeps you out in the midday sun.

Polo you can begin when the heat of the day is over, and it enables you to get your exercise and enjoyment in time to turn up at the club—that essential feature of Indian life—and to see your friends before dinner. That is why the game of kings is gradually ousting the king of games.

Also, you want a short game because India is a land of work—of increasingly hard work.

Again, if, as at Bombay, you play in the monsoon, the wickets, baked by a hot sun after heavy daily rain, are just a bit of glue, and give the batsman no fun, while the bowlers feel the effect of the burning, exhausting sun, and quickly modify their run, lose their sting, and as the phrase goes, soon bowl only twelve annas to the rupee.

If, on the other hand, you play in the cold weather, you cannot, without very great expense and trouble in watering, provide a tolerable grass wicket at all.

CECIL HEADLAM.

Lord Harris on Indian Cricket ◠

IT has been charged against British administrators that their policy in India is *Divide et impera* ; but there is no need for the British Raj to try to divide ; the natives of India do that most effectively of their own motion in matters of far more serious moment than cricket. But however great the difficulties of finance, of caste, and of climate be, there is one dominating factor which must make cricket the most popular game in India, must keep it so, and must extend it throughout the land, and that is the vivid keenness of all races and castes for the game. In out-of-the-way villages of the Mofussil you will find the boys playing with the crudest implements : and to see a crowd on the *maidan* at Bombay watching an important match is a revelation. Thousands of spectators sit and stand —unrestricted by policemen or ropes—absorbed by the game, and most intelligently approving the strokes that deserve applause. I am thankful to be able to feel sure that England has done much, very much, for India ; and one of the many good things she has done has been to introduce a manly game which is open to poor as well as rich, which needs no prize beyond honour, and by its simple merits can enlist the support and countenance of the wisest men of each religion and each caste.

MISCELLANEA

A Few Dates ✿ ✿ ✿ ✿

THE oldest existing County Club is the Surrey County Club, founded in 1844. Then come Derbyshire, 1845. Sussex, 1857. Kent and Notts, 1859. Yorkshire, 1863. Lancashire, 1864. Middlesex, 1868, and Gloucestershire, 1870.

Cricket Superstitions ✿ ✿ ✿

EVERY ONE may know the laws of cricket who will take the trouble to study the elaborate code in which they are embodied. But these are a trifle too numerous and too complicated for junior players, who therefore often seem to play cricket according to some unwritten traditional code of their own. Those who have watched small boys at play will know what I mean. Of course, I am not referring to the junior forms of public schools, amongst whom cricket is usually the genuine thing, so far as it goes. They have the authority of their seniors to appeal to in any difficulty. I am referring to those less formal games which boys, and sometimes men, get up among themselves, and which seem to be governed in many respects by certain inherited traditions. Those who have ever watched such a game will have been amused by some of these traditions.

206

For instance, it is widely believed amongst boy-cricketers that a batsman cannot be out from a ball which did not pitch half-way up the wicket. As a means of discouraging 'sneaks' and 'daisy-cutters,' this tradition has, no doubt, its value, but as yet it has found no place in the rules of the M.C.C. It may, of course, be said that the necessity for it has not, up to the present time, arisen in first-class cricket. Still, there are only two kinds of 'no-ball' possible in cricket—the one when the bowler passes the crease before delivering it, the other when he throws it. Subject to these exceptions, he has the fullest freedom to deliver the ball as he likes, and, if Mr. A. G. Steel is right, he ought, when a batsman has 'collared' the scientific bowling, to try the effect of what may be called unconventional balls. A full pitch tossed high in the air, and dropping on the bails, has been known to terminate the innings of a batsman who had defied all other attacks ; and it is possible that an occasional swift 'sneak' might prove embarrassing to a man who had not so much as seen one for, say, a dozen years. I present the suggestion to Lohmann and Attewell ; for, after all, the object of bowling is not to secure accuracy of pitch, or a brave show of 'maidens,' but to take wickets, and anything within the laws of the game that will lead to this result is not only allowable but praiseworthy. It is the fashion, for instance, to laugh at underhand bowling, but, just because this is now out of date, it sometimes proves very fatal to men who are not used to it, and therefore deserves to be tried more often than it is in ordinary matches.

In connection with 'no-balls,' juvenile cricketers

are more logical than their seniors. On the face of it, there does seem to be a certain contradiction in the fact that you may score any number of runs you can off a ball which is hypothetically a nonentity. It is an axiom of boy-cricket that this may not be done. A ' no-ball ' is a ' no-ball,' and no runs can be made off it, according to their code. As regards ' wides,' they are orthodox in theory, though somewhat amusing in practice, it being a common thing to hear the umpire call ' wide ' to a ball which the batsman promptly proceeds to hit.

But perhaps the most comical superstition in boy-cricket is that the batsman is out if he chance to hit the ball with the wrong side of his bat. This would seem to be one of those contingencies for which it was not necessary to provide a rule—at any rate, no such rule appears in the written code. One would like to know if anyone had ever seen a real cricketer make this mistake, but if he did, he would be within his right. I imagine that if a lunatic chose to play the ball with the handle of his bat, instead of with the blade, he might do so. The bowler would, I am sure, lodge no objection, though I hardly think that such a batsman would be greatly pressed by his own side to give his services in the return match.

Another curious superstition in juvenile cricket is that, if in running you drop your bat, you are out, no matter how safely you yourself may reach the crease. There is something logical in this too. A batsman is not a batsman without his bat. Following naturally on this, is the idea that a batsman is not out if his bat is grounded inside the crease and is in contact with any part of his person, whilst he himself is out of his ground. It happened once, I believe, in first-class cricket that a batsman, stepping out of the crease to hit at a ball slipped and fell down out of his ground, whilst the bat dropped from his hand. He was promptly stumped, but, as the bat was within the crease and was in contact with his elbow, the umpire gave him 'not out.' He was wrong; the bat must be in the hand to save the batsman's life in these circumstances.

If we were to philosophize on such superstitions, we should perhaps be inclined to say that the main characteristic of juvenile cricketers is that they are essentially matter-of-fact. With them a ' no-ball ' is a ' no-ball '; ' hit wicket ' means hitting the wicket at any time; a batsman is a man who has actually a bat in his hand, and so on. Another instance of this matter-of-fact spirit is the way in which juvenile cricketers regard the ' leg before wicket ' rule. With them, no allowance is made, no matter how ' curly ' the ball may be. If your leg is before the wicket, and the ball hits your leg, it is all over with you. *Bad* players may be tolerated, but no mercy is shown to *pad* players.

A. E. EVANS.

The Champagne of Cricket ✎ ✎

I THINK the most memorable sight I ever witnessed upon a cricket-field was that of Spofforth and S. M. J. Woods (the two fastest amateur bowlers of their day) sharing the attack, to the batting of Gunn and Shrewsbury, and the wicket-keeping of Gregor McGregor. Now that *was* the champagne of cricket, and Grace in his palmiest days never showed a bolder front (and to such bowling !) than those two Nottingham men did to the Australian-born and the Australian-bred. Only when Hobbs has been giving an exhibition of *his* particular prowess at the Oval have I seen enthusiasm to equal it. My second ' best ' was, I think, the 500 for two wickets of Gentlemen *v.* Players at Lord's in 1904, when I saw C. B. Fry score upwards of 200, A. C. Maclaren 160, and ' Ranji ' 60.

PERCY CROSS STANDING.

' W. G.' to Phil May

(On a *Punch* Cartoon)

WHY, oh why did you give ' square-leg ' wicket-keeper's gloves when you showed us 'Arry at the wicket ? My sons (who are cricketers also) demanded an explanation of me last evening at dinner. ' Oh,' said I, ' to counteract 'Arry's evident violent play.' But they were not satisfied, and wanted to know why some of the spectators were wearing overcoats ? ' For the same reason,' said I.

[The late Phil May replied, ' *To keep his hands warm.*']

Humours of Umpiring

THE finest thing in umpiring was ' made a note of ' in Central Bucks the other day, in a village match, between two teams above village average in both play and knowledge of the game. This amazing umpire, *after a single run* had been scored by two players who made no attempt to run again, shouted

' Short run ! ' Shouts of laughter from the umpire's own side caused him hastily to withdraw his verdict, but it will never be forgotten, even in the village play of those rural shades.

At a cricket match played last summer in Yorkshire, a batsman was given out ' leg before wicket,' much to his dissatisfaction. ' Well,' said the umpire who had given him out, ' if tha' doesn't believe me, just come to this end and see where thy foot is for thysen.'

The First Canterbury Week, 1842

YOUR cricketer no cogging practice knows,
No trick to favour friends or cripple foes ;
His motto still is : ' May the best man win.'
Let Sussex boast her *Taylor*, Kent her *Mynn*,
Your cricketer, right English to the core,
Still loves the man best he has licked before.

TOM TAYLOR.

The Third Stump

THE precise year in which the third stump was introduced is unknown. The *Hampshire Chronicle* of September 7, 1776, gives an account of a match played with three stumps, while Nyren gives the date as 1779 or 1780. In point of fact, and unless artists were in error, the old method lingered for years. In the Willett collection of pottery, in the Brighton Museum, is a mug of Staffordshire creamware which has on it a representation of a match played between M.C.C. and Kent, at Lord's, June 20 and 21, 1793, in which only two stumps were

P

used. On the other hand, in Richard Wilson's painting of a cricket match at Moulsey Hurst, three stumps are shown. No date is attached to the painting under notice; but it is an undisputed fact that R. Wilson, R.A., died in 1782.

A. D. TAYLOR.

The Value of Fielding ∽   ∽   ∽

1. STUDY yourself the art of hitting fielding practice—you cannot do it if you hold the bat with two hands.
2. Teach every man first of all the right way to hold his hands for fielding and catching and the right way to place his feet. There is a right way, and there are several wrong ways.
3. Make all the fielders be on the move towards you as you hit the ball.
4. Hit the ball, whether along the ground or in the air, so that the fielder has to cover ground to get it.
5. Insist on a second man backing up the fieldsman.
6. Teach every man the right way to throw the ball in.
7. Give all the fielders practice for nearly all the positions in the field, but give some special practice in a particular position.
8. Vary your method of hitting the ball and making it bounce direct from the bat.
9. Give long high catches to those only (as few as possible) who may be required to field in the outfield.

10. Spend some time each fielding practice in getting the men round you in a circle and hitting the ball to them from full pitch returns on to the front or back of the bat.

11. See your slip fielders have continual practice from balls thrown on to the back of three bats fixed together, a roller, or one of the specially constructed racks.

12. Teach all your men to raise themselves on their toes as each ball is hit so that they start the quicker.

13. Above all, see that you vary the form of practice, and keep up the interest of all the fieldsmen.

G. N. FOSTER.

Cricket Colloquialisms ∽ ∽ ∽

ON BEING BOWLED

'MY dear fellow, can't think how I missed it. Easiest ball ever saw in my life.'

'Worst wicket I ever came across. Wouldn't play there again if you paid me.'

'Umpire slick behind his arm ; couldn't see a bit.'

'Filthy thing shot and broke half a yard.'

'Never tried to play it—feel rather seedy—glad to get out.'

'Best ball of the match, sir ! ' (*N.B.—Especially if you are out first.*)

'I hope none of you chaps'll get another like it.'

'This brings my average down horrid.' (*N.B.— This only when you have made at least 50 runs.*)

On Being Caught

'I'll swear it was a bump-ball, if I never speak again.'

'I never went within a yard of it! You heard it!! Why, that was a man chopping wood in the next field.'

'I *never* get let off by any chance.'

'Haven't been missed this year.'

'First ball I've lifted off the ground for two seasons. Caught last week, was I? Given *out* caught, you mean; quite another thing, my boy.'

'I shall chuck cricket—no more luck than a cat. As many lives have I? Well, how many have I had to-day, pray?'

'Devilish good hit; would have been out of any ordinary ground.'

'This infernal bat don't drive a little bit.'

On Being Run Out

'No use playing against an umpire!'

'The old beast was looking the other way.'

'I swear I was past the wicket; there's my heelmarks to prove it.'

''Twasn't his call at all, the fool.'

'I swear I won't go in with Brown again.'

'Oh, it's no use if Jones *will* run for the ball, don't you know?'

On Being Leg Before Wicket

'No one but a cad would have asked such a thing.'

'Umpire means to earn his money, at any rate. *Our* umpire, is he? Well, all I can say is, he's an old fool.'

' It hit me on the back of my head ! '

' I've the mark on my elbow ! Same mark you saw before I went in ? Bosh ! You must have been drunk.'

' I hit it hard.'

' I'm hanged if I'll ever touch a bat again.'

' Pitched wide of the off stump, and broke a foot.'

' Well, I've kneecap-itulated to the inevitable ! ' (N.B.—*This formula is only available when you've scored over* 100 *runs.*)

On Being Stumped

' Well, all I can say is, I never moved my foot.'

' Umpire be d——d ! '

On Missing a Catch

' The sun was bang in my eyes.'

' Funny thing—never missed one before that I can remember.'

' First this season, my boy : more than you can say.'

' Good Gad ! there *was* a lot of spin on that ball.'

' Right on my old sore place.'

' Shouldn't call that a chance, should *you* ? '

On Being Taken Off Bowling

' I'd just found the right length too.'

' Well, they didn't get many runs off *me*.'

' Captain, indeed ! He isn't fit to black boots !

' First time this year I haven't got six wickets.'

' Well, one can't bowl a hat *every* innings.'

' Mind you, I was bowling thundering well.'

' What's the use if fellows can't hold catches ? '

' Quite the worst bats I ever saw.'

' Hate bowling with a sticky ball.'

' I'd have *asked* to be taken off at the proper time.'

' Well, I shan't play for the Bottlejugs again ! '

WILLIAM SAPTE.

Indiscriminate Charity ⌒ ⌒

BENEVOLENT old lady : ' No, Mr. Smith, I shall not continue my subscription to your cricket-ground any longer, for I find you allow it to be used in the winter for pigeon-shooting.'

Secretary to the local Cricket Club : ' But, madam, you can't be aware that we shoot at nothing but *clay* pigeons ! '

B.O.L. : ' I don't care what the breed may be,— it's equally cruel ! '

Concerning Collapses ⌒ ⌒ ⌒

WHEN a good eleven, or one which is thought good is got rid of for a small score, one cricketer after another who has not been present is apt to bombard those who were with the question, ' I say, how do you explain that collapse the other day ? ' Now a good judge of the game, who has been following it carefully, can often throw some light on what has happened, by describing how the wickets changed in character or how a sudden gloom over-spread the evening sky, and so forth. But in the majority of these cases collapses are not to be explained by any such reason at all. Let us consider the plain law of averages. Take any batsman, and watch him through five or six matches when he is in full practice ; once at least he will get out for a

very small score in that time in a way that he can't
explain. He was bowled by a good ball or caught
off a bad hit, and there's an end of it. Excepting
under very exceptional circumstances the above
would hold good of any cricketer. Now, an eleven
plays together throughout the year. Suppose
there are six batsmen on whom they mainly depend,
is it not clear that in all probability once or twice
at least in the course of the season the bad days of
those six batsmen will coincide? It would, anyhow,
be strange if they did not. The sort of eleven to
whom it is least likely to happen is one like the
Australians.

THE HON. REV. E. LYTTELTON.

The Learner's Art ᗡ ᗡ ᗡ

SCARCELY any school nowadays is without some
master, probably himself a well-known cricketer,
who devotes his spare time to bowling at the nets
to his young pupils and giving them advice. Many
of us acquired the rudiments of the game at the
teaching of kindly mentors like these, and nobody
can deny that all interested in cricket owe a very
decided debt of gratitude to those who thus
voluntarily give the benefit of their experience
and example to young players who have not yet
lost the capacity of learning.

Two Repton Captains ᗡ ᗡ ᗡ

WHEN I went to Repton, the captain of cricket
was Mr. F. G. J. Ford, the great Middlesex batsman.
He was a magnificent school cricketer, and I can
remember watching him from the paddock bank

in distant reverence. Mr. L. C. H. Palairet got
into the Repton team in my first summer ; he was
quite a small boy, but played in beautiful style.
My first sphere of action was the fourth ground,
where we played pick-up matches on half-holidays
and had net practice on the principle of ' you
batted if you bowled the man out.' In my third
year, when Mr. L. C. H. Palairet was captain, I
got my cricket colours. My chief merit was being
able to stick in, for I was a marvellously stiff
player and could not bat a bit except on the leg
side. This stiffness was due, I believe, to the mis-
conception that the art of batting consisted entirely
in playing forward. I used to tie myself up into
extraordinary knots trying to play forward at un-
suitable balls.

C. B. FRY.

Batting and Betting at Canterbury, 1842

THERE were four or five good ' hands ' made in
that match, Kent v. England, and so there were
against us. Mr. Felix and I and Alfred Mynn
were in pretty near a whole day against eight
bowlers, and over 750 balls were bowled in the
first ' hand.' Tom Barker and Joseph Guy made
the long hands for England, and our side bowled
almost as many balls. Kent got 278, England 206,
and then the ground was so cut up that Lillywhite
and Dean, without a change, got the lot of us for
44 in our second hands, and England won by nine
wickets. When we got to 278, one of the Kentish
farmers offered 30 to 1 in sovereigns on Kent, and
an officer at Canterbury took him four times over,

and old ' top-boots ' did sigh when he went home for his canvas bag to pay up. Yet these farmers were not contented unless they had from one to five pounds on their own county.

FULLER PILCH.

On Wicket-Keeping

THERE is probably no hope of getting a really good man out on a good wicket, which can be compared to the chance of his sending a catch to the wicket-keeper before his eye is in. Sometimes these chances are missed, and no one notices anything; but even of those noticed the number is enormous, far greater than that which any other single field holds or drops—indeed, on hard, smooth wickets almost as great as that of all the other fields put together. And yet an eleven will go smiling into the field without a (practised) wicket-keeper! Everybody thinks it will come right somehow; so it does, but the match is first lost. Of course the regular wicket-keeper's *practice* of his art must be limited by consideration for his hands. Even allowing for this, it is probable that he would gain if he devoted some time every day merely to taking the slow balls and watching the fast ones. I repeat that familiarity with the motion of the ball is enormously important. But every member of any team would gain if he were taught how to keep wickets in early youth. In the first place, it certainly helps the eye in batting. The problem of judging pace, pitch, and break is exactly the same in both cases. Next, it teaches sureness of hand in fielding. A field who has learnt wicket-keeping must find any catch, especially if it does not involve running, mere child's play compared with a chance behind the sticks. It is impossible that any such continuous exercise of hand and eye of the most subtle description could be anything but valuable to the general quickness and sureness both of fielding and batting. Lastly, even if all the eleven do not learn how to keep wickets, there ought always to be one or more ready to take the place of the regular man, in case of injury or absence.

THE HON. THE REV. E. LYTTELTON.

A Royal Match of 1735

A GREAT match at Cricket has been made between His Royal Highness the Prince of Wales and the Earl of Middlesex for £1,000. Eight of the London club and three out of Middlesex are to play for the Prince against Eleven to be chosen by the Earl out of Kent: they are to play twice—viz., at Moulsey Hurst next Saturday, and afterwards at Dartford in Kent. . . .

Yesterday at the cricket match on Bromly Common between the Prince of Wales and the Earl of Middlesex for £1,000, the Londoners got 72 the first hands, the Kentish men 95. London side went in again and got only nine above the Kent, which were got the second hands without one person's being out, by the Kentish men, who won the match.

George IV as Cricketer

THE Prince of Wales (afterwards George IV) was exceedingly fond of cricket. In 1791 he had a marquee erected on his newly-formed cricket ground at Brighton, in which it is recorded he dined *seven* days in succession. He played cricket, we are told, with ' great condescension and affability.' Lord Barrymore was a bosom friend of the Prince, and a great patron of the game. When Lord Barrymore came of age (in 1790) he inherited £20,000 a year ; but his losses on the turf and elsewhere in the first year after obtaining his fortune were so great that he vowed he would give up racing altogether. He was the eldest of three brothers, all of whom were a dare-devil set, their sister surpassing in deeds of recklessness the whole three. She was president of the ' Hellfire Club,' of which they were all members. A. D. TAYLOR.

The Puzzled Foreigner ⌒ ⌒ ⌒

' I DO not understand your crickets,' said a foreigner to me ; ' To me it do appear that it proceed upon wrong principle—that you are what you call penalized when you make the good stroke. For when you make the good stroke you do have to start away and run like the diable. But it should be the man who plays badly—he should run and the man who plays well, rest. Instead of which, death of my life ! it is the man that gets what you call bowled out who is allowed to sit himself in the pavilion all the afternoon, in the shade, and enjoy himself.'

HORACE G. HUTCHINSON.

Jerks in from Short-Leg ⌒ ⌒

THE requirements of the cricket profession may be very shortly summed up :

'Natural gifts, attended by regularity of habits.' No professional drunkard has ever made a great professional cricketer, nor ever will. . . .

Are there not latterly rumours of disagreements, divisions, and petty jealousies amongst our ' peaceful brethren of the willow ? ' We have heard, with grief, of a split in our Cricket Family, and with one of its most attached relations. It is not our province to probe the wound, we are averse even to prescribing any course of treatment ; we should like to see the wound healed ; and wherever and whenever we can introduce some of our ' nostrums ' without fear of being considered a quack, but with a view to allay the existing irritation, we intend to do so. It is far from our intention to dissuade any aspirants from joining the profession ; as a class we have a great respect for the professors, and we have known very few instances where the Raw Material—picked up on the hills of Surrey, the plains of Cambridge, amidst the smoke of Nottingham, among the pits of Yorkshire—has not been converted into very useful, if not ornamental, members of society. . . .

Cricket is a very trying game, and really if we hadn't ourselves the temper of many angels we should have given it up long ago. We imagine there must be something indescribably seductive in the reaction ; that the devil, when cast out in the form of heated expletive, leaves the system in that deliciously soothened state which we read of in the advertisements of the Turkish Baths. One great mystery to us is—Why does an irascible bowler ever bowl at all ? It doesn't improve him *not to ask him* to bowl, although he is sure to ' rise ' if he does.

We are far from wishing there should be no temper at all ; it smartens up a listless field amazingly, and it very often provokes mirth. We only think, in analysing the reason *why* an irascible man plays cricket, that he cannot feel a real pleasure : but we must be wrong, as there are so many irascibles who devote themselves to the game. We conclude they look upon it much as the engine-driver does on his safety-valve—if they hadn't the open air and the excuse (which cricket certainly admits of) for a good volley of expletives, what would become of the china and other personal property in their domestic circles ; on the whole, therefore, we are inclined to believe that the irascibles owe a deep debt of gratitude to cricket, for affording them a semi-legitimate vent for those feelings which would not otherwise be conducive to the comfort of a home, or the proper organization of the breakfast table.

A Cricket Umpire's Dream

AT Eccleshall, near Sheffield, there was formerly a parish clerk called Lingard, who was also a notable umpire. One hot Sunday he was asleep at his desk and was dreaming about a match to be played the next day. After the sermon, when the time came for him to utter his customary ' Amen ' he surprised the preacher and delighted the rustics who were present by shouting in a loud voice the word ' Over.'

Cricket and Exercise in General ✍

THE fine, hard, flat, verdant floors are now preparing in the cricket-grounds for this manly and graceful game, and the village-greens (where they can) are no less getting ready, though not quite so perfect. No matter for that. A true cricketer is not the man to be put out by a trifle. He serves an apprenticeship to patience after her handsomest fashion. Henry the Fourth wished a time might arrive in France when every man should have a pullet in his kettle. We should like to see a time when every man played at cricket, and had a sound sleep after it, and health, work, and leisure. It would be a pretty world, if we all had something to do, just to make leisure the pleasanter, and green merry England were sprinkled all over, ' of afternoons,' with gallant fellows in white sleeves, who threshed the earth and air of their cricket-grounds into a crop of health and spirits ; after which they should read, laugh, love, and be honourable and happy beings, bringing God's work to its perfection, and suiting the divine creation they live in.

But to speak in this manner is to mix serious things with mirthful. Well ; and what true joy does not ? Joy, if you did but know him thoroughly, is a very serious fellow—on occasion ; and knows that happiness is a very solid thing, and is jealous for nature's honour and glory. The power to be grave is the proper foundation for levity itself to rejoice on. You must have floor for your dancing— good solid earth on which to bother your cricket-balls.

The Spring is monstrously said to be a sickly time

of the year. Yes, for the sickly ; or rather (not to speak irreverently of sickness which cannot be helped) for those who have suffered themselves to become so for want of stirring their bloods, and preparing for the general movement in Nature's merry veins. People stop indoors, and render themselves liable to all ' the skiey influences ' and then out of the same thoughtless effeminacy of self-indulgence, they expose themselves to the catching of colds and fevers, and the beautiful Spring is blamed, and ' fine Mays make fat church-yards.' The gipsies, we will be bound, have no such proverb. The cricketer has none such. He is a sensible, hearty fellow, too wise not to take proper precautions, but above all, too wise not to take the best of all precautions ; which is, to take care of his health, and be stirring. Nature is stirring, and so is he. Nature, in a hundred thousand parts to a fraction, is made up of air, and fields, and country, and out-of-doors, and a strong teeming earth, and a good-natured sky ; and so is the strong heart of the cricketer.

LEIGH HUNT.